THE DEREK CROSS COLLECTION

THE SOUTHERN IN TRANSITION
1946–1966

Front cover:
Early June 1960 sees unrebuilt Bulleid 'West Country' pacific No. 34091 *Weymouth* at Petts Wood. The train is the most prestigious in the timetable: the 'Golden Arrow' from London to Paris via Dover. British Railways Southern Region steam in its pomp some sixty-two years ago now!

Back cover top:
Class O1 No. 31258, already sixty-six years old in April 1960, is pictured busy at work in the Kent coalfield. Allocated to Dover shed the locomotive, which was new in 1894, and brake van are heading to the colliery at Tilmanstone for another load of coal. The period road signs and the huge telegraph pole add to the scene.

Back cover bottom:
At Cranbrook station, on the Hawkhurst branch, in May 1960, we see a school special about to set off. The locomotive is a Maunsell 'D1' class No. 31749.

THE DEREK CROSS COLLECTION

THE SOUTHERN IN TRANSITION 1946–1966

DAVID CROSS

Pen & Sword TRANSPORT

AN IMPRINT OF PEN & SWORD BOOKS LTD.
YORKSHIRE – PHILADELPHIA

First published in Great Britain in 2022 by
Pen and Sword Transport
An imprint of
Pen & Sword Books Ltd.
Yorkshire - Philadelphia

Copyright © David Cross, 2022

ISBN 978 1 52675 490 5

The right of David Cross to be identified as author of this work has been asserted by him in accordance with the Copyright, Designs and Patents Act 1988.

A CIP catalogue record for this book is available from the British Library.

All rights reserved. No part of this book may be reproduced or transmitted in any form or by any means, electronic or mechanical including photocopying, recording or by any information storage and retrieval system, without permission from the Publisher in writing.

Typeset in 11/13 Palatino by SJmagic DESIGN SERVICES, India.

Printed and bound by Printworks Global Ltd, London/Hong Kong.

Pen & Sword Books Ltd incorporates the imprints of Pen & Sword Books Archaeology, Atlas, Aviation, Battleground, Discovery, Family History, History, Maritime, Military, Naval, Politics, Railways, Select, Transport, True Crime, Fiction, Frontline Books, Leo Cooper, Praetorian Press, Seaforth Publishing, Wharncliffe and White Owl.

For a complete list of Pen & Sword titles please contact

PEN & SWORD BOOKS LIMITED
47 Church Street, Barnsley, South Yorkshire, S70 2AS, England
E-mail: enquiries@pen-and-sword.co.uk
Website: www.pen-and-sword.co.uk

or

PEN AND SWORD BOOKS
1950 Lawrence Rd, Havertown, PA 19083, USA
E-mail: Uspen-and-sword@casematepublishers.com
Website: www.penandswordbooks.com

CONTENTS

Introduction 6

South Eastern Division 12

South Central Division 76

South Western Division 104

INTRODUCTION

Pictured at Victoria station in the autumn of 1951 is my Mother and Derek's wife, Elizabeth Cross. It had to be a railway background didn't it and quite some background! An immaculate 'Britannia' *William Shakespeare* waits to depart with the down 'Golden Arrow'. My Mother died during the writing of this book in April 2020 aged ninety-six and I'm pleased to include this picture in her memory.

Let me surprise you! My late father, Derek Cross, whose pictures make up 99% of the photographs in this book, was a man of Kent! Although well known for his 'train in the landscape' style of railway photography in the high hills and fells of Scotland and north-west England his first love was the Southern. For that reason I am delighted to have put together this book, *The Southern in Transition*, using his pictures in a part of the country for which he had great affection.

Derek was born at Hythe in Kent in 1929 and spent much of his childhood in Kent. He went to school locally, his grandparents lived in nearby Folkestone, and after secondary school he returned to Kent to study at the then Imperial College campus at Wye College, just a few miles from where he had grown up. It was another local attraction, literally on his doorstep, that we believe led him to have such a long lasting interest in railways. Captain Howey had set up the Romney, Hythe & Dymchurch fifteen-inch gauge railway from Hythe through New Romney to Dungeness in 1926. The RH&DR was reportedly the Kent main line in miniature and its locomotive No. 1 *Green Goddess* named after a

INTRODUCTION • 7

Ian Allan ABCs the must have for those with an interest in railways for generations! Derek Cross was no different and this picture of the front cover of his copy of ABC Number 2 confirms this. Inside typically there is lots of underlining, red and blue ink. After all those years, I still refer to it from time to time and SR 'Schools' class *St Olave's* is on the cover! This locomotive also features in this book recorded on the Royal Train!

Mentioned in the text, we know Derek's interest in railways was nurtured by trips from his home in Hythe to the then infant Romney, Hythe & Dymchurch Railway. For that reason I'm including a picture at his 'home station' of Hythe. Taken in 1959 we see an enthusiast in 'period dress' admiring RHDR No. 2 *Southern Maid*. This was always a line he enjoyed very much and later it was managed by his friend from New Zealand days, the late John Snell.

play Captain Howey liked! Reportedly Derek loved going there from a very early age and made several trips to the railway, making an impression on him as a small boy through the thirties. During this time he became familiar with Pacifics, coaching stock, semaphore signals, double track main lines and the all-important steam locomotive, and how it all worked. He had got the bug. As a teenager through the war years when at his age many of us were experimenting – in my case, with an Ilford Sporti camera and Selochrome Pan film! – he had little opportunity to do the same because there were few cameras for sale and no film to speak of. After the end of the war and with Nationalisation the Southern Railway gradually became the Southern Region of the infant British Railways. At this time Derek was also changing from being a railway enthusiast to a railway photographer. The immediate evidence of this was when he went to Wye College and there are literally dozens and dozens of pictures taken in and around Wye station and several on the SR line from Ashford through Wye to Minster. A number of these are included in this book because they are so interesting in terms of locomotives, combinations, liveries and train formations, all over seventy years ago now. If the quality of the pictures is not quite as you might expect in today's digital world then please forgive me.

In those days the available cameras were both limited and expensive. A number of people have asked what cameras Derek used and from what I can gather – bearing in mind that the early pictures were taken before I was born! – it seems that the very early pictures were taken using a 35mm Voigtlander Bessa. There was also an Agfa Record 120 size film camera which took just eight 2¼ x 3¼ large negatives per roll of film. The film seems to have been predominantly Ilford – mainly black and white negatives. The early pictures used a brand called 'Panchromatic Hypersensitive Fine Grain' and later on brands with which we all became familiar such as Ilford FP3 and HP3. From the very late fifties Derek bought a large press camera made by Linhof with interchangeable backs, which he liked very much, and helped him to take account of changing weather conditions, and which I'll hope you agree, produced some very good results as day-to-day steam entered its last decade on the Southern Region.

Derek Cross was most at home in the countryside and was a champion of the train in the landscape as I have already mentioned. We believe this was in part because of his geological training, which began at Wye College and which we think influenced this style. Surrey and the south coast counties of Kent, Sussex, Hampshire and Dorset lend themselves to this type of photography and I'm pleased to share over 200 images that Derek took in this area between 1948 and 1967. From 1952 for around five years Derek went to work in New Zealand as a geologist, moving first to Wellington and then to Rotorua. I was born during his stay in New Zealand and was present as a very young boy when some of the pictures were taken in the sixties, as you can see in pictures at Coombe Road, Fleet and Upwey Wishing Well. Later on I would more regularly join my father on his photographic expeditions, for that is what they were! The day before the planned trip weather forecasts would be listened to on the radio, British Railways contacts telephoned and an armful of timetables and Special Traffic Notices placed in the car. If all was well it was early to bed to set off the next day at five in the morning. In those days radio did not operate during the night and I have vivid memories of listening to Handel's *Water Music*, which was played when the BBC Home Service opened I think at 6am! Once on the way a very structured plan was followed, taking advantage of the position of the sun in relation to the railway line, the times the interesting trains were due and where we had planned to have lunch. I still have many of the Ordnance Survey maps with arrows and squiggles on them, identifying a good photographic spot: 'am or pm, up or down'. Many of these trips on the Southern were with his friends Gordon Boland, John Snell (who later ran the RH&DR), Chris Haes, Tom Wright, Ted Woollard (who has two pictures in this book) and Stanley Creer, and a man whose proper name I do not recall but he was known as Mr Pest! To this day I don't know why this was his nickname. For trips to the West Country Ivo Peters, Norman Lockett and Ossie Nock often joined us. On some occasions some of Derek's team was substituted by my mother, my brother and me, all given cameras to use and actually all of us had pictures published, even if it was black and white in the *Meccano Magazine*! The trips were often all-day affairs and I remember getting squeezed into Derek's sky blue MG Magnette registration number VVB 321: his pride and joy at the time! I seem to recall the dress code for adults was jackets and ties in those days. For readers, shall we say of less than state pension age today, I'd guess all this seems to be impossible to believe! However, to go back sixty years, the only way of communicating amongst friends or with information was face-to-face, by letter or by landline telephone. In our house even the telephone was not our own as it was shared with a neighbour on something called a 'party line'. This meant that if House A was on the phone House B could not use the phone but could, should you be so inclined, listen in to the other conversation. Add to this no digital camera equipment, film, that at 125 ASA was fast and the vagaries of the British weather, I think it's a miracle they obtained the photographs and the quality of photographs that they did. Indeed, sharing these pictures after all the trouble Derek went to is one of the motivations for me to write this book.

Back to Derek and his love of the Southern Railway and Southern Region of British Railways. I have unearthed an extract, he wrote, which explains the reasons in his own words.

> 'The scent of ripe apples, the outline of oast houses and above all the warmth of the sun on one's back; these are my principal childhood memories of my native county of Kent. Only maturing years have brought back the smell of burning leaves in autumn around Shorncliffe station and the wet mists of the Weald in winter. Other odours from my childhood recollections were the sulphurous smell of Kent coal drifting from locomotives at Charing Cross or billowing through my grandmother's garden near Shorncliffe from the main line to the coast. The fascination of the railways of Kent that I grew up with spread through the years to cover the whole of what became the Southern Region. What was the fascination of the Southern in steam days that set it apart from any other company? Not least was the endless variety of its motive power right through into the early sixties, also the fact that these locomotives tended to be used on a single, first-come, first-served, basis whereby a modern Pacific was quite likely to be followed some minutes later by a 4-4-0 of advancing years on a goods train. Another facet of the Southern charm was the country it served once out of the suburbs of south and west London. Most of the lines ran through a countryside almost wanton in its loveliness. Hilaire Belloc's "great hills of the south country" were never far away. It was a system of trees and colour of cider and cherries. It also contained a number of lines that were hard on its locomotives; for example the gruelling climb out of Weymouth through Upwey (steeper than Shap and nearly as long) and the grades up to Mortehoe in North Devon, which were without parallel for what was once a very busy line in summertime. Even the main line from Salisbury to the west had a profile like the teeth of a badly sharpened saw, and the Portsmouth direct line from Woking was little better. The Chatham line to Dover was all curves with some short sharp gradients thrown in, and if anything the South Eastern was worse, with climb through the North Downs by way of Knockholt forming the hardest start of any main line out of London.'

I sincerely hope that much of what Derek said about 'the Southern' I have been able to cover and illustrate in this book. As Derek said there was huge variety in scenery and in locomotives and I hope I have organised the book in roughly the same way as the railway companies did. The three Southern Region operating divisions were geographical but were largely structured along the lines of each of the pre-grouping companies that had formed the Southern Railway. The SE&CR became the basis for the Eastern Division, the L&SWR the Western Division and, in the middle, the LB&SCR the Central Division. This book is laid out starting with the Eastern Division, followed by the Central Division and finally the Western Division. Generally the Eastern section was probably the busiest and most varied; this is reflected in the picture selections in part, because it was the busiest and in part, because it was closest to where we lived in Croydon. The Central section was principally a number of secondary main lines and some fascinating branch lines roughly in a triangle between Tonbridge, Hastings and Portsmouth. The main stem of this triangle was the former LB&SCR between London and Brighton. The last part of the book, the Western section, covered the lines of the former LS&WR. This area is easier to define, in four words; Southampton/Weymouth and Exeter/Plymouth, but having said that it was no less interesting.

    Finally, if I may, a tribute to my mother, Elizabeth Cross, Derek's wife for over thirty years, who sadly passed away during the preparation of this book in April 2020. She was ninety-six and I guess may have been to more railway stations than any other woman! She was very patient and very supportive of our hobby, encouraging my brother and me to go on these photographic expeditions with Derek . … perhaps to give her some peace at home in Croydon, where we lived at the time! My interest endured, that of my brother less so. Another Mrs Cross, my wife Jane, also deserves a mention for her patience and assistance with compiling this book, as does my friend, Peter Waller who has also been a great help. There is no bibliography to speak of as ninety-nine per cent of this book is Cross family material! However, I would like to mention the two reference books written by Hugh Longworth as being a valuable source of data. The respected railway journalist Rex Kennedy commented in his magazine some months ago that there is nothing more rewarding for a father and son than to enjoy a shared interest. In railway photography this seems quite common with Rex and his children, Henry and Richard Casserley, Geoff Bannister and his son and Derek and me.

    I do hope that you enjoy this book and Derek's wonderful pictures.

David Cross
Brentwood,
May 2022

SOUTH EASTERN DIVISION

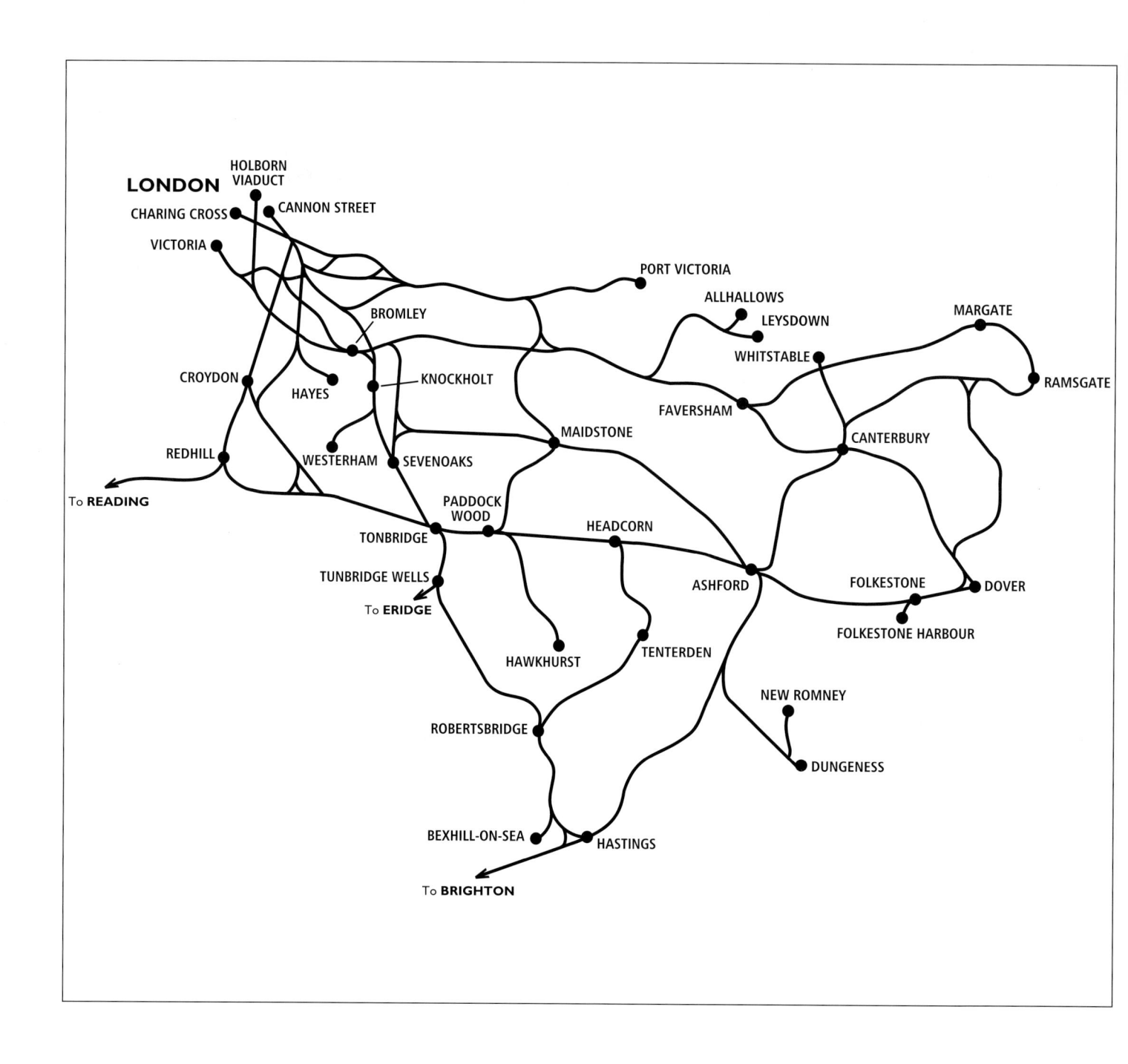

SOUTH EASTERN DIVISION • 13

The builder's plate on this Ivatt 2-6-2T indicates that it had been built at Crewe in 1951, just six months before this picture was taken in June 1952. The locomotive was new to Bricklayers Arms shed and here we see No. 41299 engaged in station pilot duties at Charing Cross station. Derek records the train as empty coaching stock from the service that had arrived from Hastings. We could perhaps guess that this was an afternoon shot, in view of the uniformed schoolboy watching proceedings. This 'schoolboy' must today be approaching his eighties!

This picture, taken at Charing Cross in August 1952, confirms the Southern Railway's addiction to signal boxes on stilts. This signal box was a very splendid structure, which Derek repeatedly said always gave him the impression was about to fall down. The train has just crossed Hungerford Bridge, one of only three bridges across the Thames that carries pedestrians and the railway only. The train from Hastings was hauled by 'Schools' class No. 30905 *Tonbridge*. The locomotive carries a 74E St Leonard's shed plate that was, of course, the local motive power depot to Hastings.

14 • THE DEREK CROSS COLLECTION: THE SOUTHERN IN TRANSITION 1946–1966

A diverted down boat train to Folkestone is pictured passing through Crystal Palace station in January 1960. Crystal Palace is approached through quite a long tunnel and there is evidence of the fireman getting to work on the fire for the gradients ahead. The train is hauled by unrebuilt 'West Country' No. 34101 *Hartland*, at that stage a couple of months short of its tenth birthday. The locomotive was rebuilt later that year and withdrawn by British Railways in 1967. Later preserved, the locomotive is now based in faraway North Yorkshire as part of the North Yorkshire Moors active steam fleet.

A nine-coach London to Margate service, diverted off its normal route, is seen near Eltham Park in June 1959. The locomotive is a Wainwright 'D1' class No. 31145, which had been built by Dübs & Co in 1903 and later rebuilt by Maunsell in the 1920s. A number of 'E' class locos were converted to 'E1s' and the 'D1' class were pretty much identical. They could only be differentiated because the 'D1s' had plain coupling rods while the 'E1s' had fluted coupling rods. By all accounts 'E1' No. 31145 was a super performer. I have a postcard exchange between Dick Riley, the much respected railway photographer, and Richard 'Dick' Hardy, the long-time shed master at Stewarts Lane, in which the latter says this loco was 'a real crack engine!' He also mentions two drivers who got the best out of the locomotive: Harry Hill of Bricklayers Arms and Dave Humphreys of Dover shed.

Monday 1 June 1959 we see BR standard Class 5 No. 73081 near Bexley with the 9.56am service from Victoria to Ramsgate. As was common at that time, there is great variety of coaching stock in the eleven-coach formation, including three Pullman cars. No. 73081 had been built at Derby in 1955 and spent its ten-year working life on the Southern Region based at Stewarts Lane, Nine Elms and Guildford. In the early sixties it was named *Excalibur*.

Rebuilt 'West Country' No. 34004 *Yeovil* emerges from the tunnel at Elmstead Woods with a service from Charing Cross to Ramsgate. The picture was taken in June 1959. No. 34004 had been rebuilt in early 1958 and allocated to Bricklayers Arms shed. Before that, in 1948, *Yeovil* had played an active and important part in the 1948 Locomotive Exchanges, even running with an LMS tender! The locomotive later migrated to the South Western Division and was withdrawn from Bournemouth shed at the end of Southern Region steam in July 1967.

16 • THE DEREK CROSS COLLECTION: THE SOUTHERN IN TRANSITION 1946–1966

Class D1 No. 31735, designed as a 'D' by Wainwright and built by Sharp Stewart in 1901 and later converted to a 'D1' by Maunsell in 1927, is pictured approaching Bromley South in June 1959. The train is an up parcels consisting mainly of PMVs; we think this was a service known as the 'Ramsgate Vans' which ran daily from Ramsgate to London Bridge.

Leaving Bromley South station in July 1959 there might be a bit of a race on between '4-SUB' EMU No. 4101 heading away from London and 'Schools' class No. 30915 *Brighton* on a relief service from London to Margate. Through the 1960s sequentially the railways went from steam to diesel to electric; however, on the Eastern Division of the Southern Region there was a very short diesel era. Steam was gradually replaced by electric traction, the biggest changeover year being 1961. This electric unit had been built in 1941 as the prototype of the new welded steel four-car suburban sets that could accommodate six seated abreast.

SOUTH EASTERN DIVISION • 17

In this May 1959 picture we see the 'Golden Arrow' approaching Bromley South heading towards London Victoria. Once through Bromley South this 'up' Golden Arrow has just 11 miles to travel. The locomotive that day was Bulleid un-rebuilt Merchant Navy pacific , 35028 "Clan Line", of Stewarts Lane shed. Later that month 35028 was transferred across London to Nine Elms. Briefly the origins of the name 'Golden Arrow' are interesting being named after a motor car which broke the world land speed record in Daytona Beach in Florida , USA in 1929 , the year Derek was born.

This April 1959 shot was recorded at Petts Wood. On the right of the picture we see a lengthy down goods hauled by 'N' class No. 31873; this is being overtaken by a Hastings DEMU No. 1033 on a service from London to Hastings. Of note in this picture are permanent way/track workers all over the place without an obvious lookout or a high visibility jacket in sight!

In this picture, taken in March 1959, Derek records this train as an 'Officers special'. It is clearly not a normal train as the fifty-six year old 'D1' No. 31749 is beautifully turned out, including burnished buffers, whilst the rest of the train shows a great variety of rolling stock with no two vehicles the same. The train is travelling in the up direction at St Mary Cray towards London, and might well be a 'top brass' inspection of progress on the electrification project.

Later in this book we will see pictures of 'hop pickers' specials' and here we see a picture of a 'pigeon special'. During the fifties virtually all travel was by train as there were very few long distance commercial vehicles. The traffic on this twelve-coach, mainly of LNER origin stock, is homing pigeons. They are being taken from Newcastle upon Tyne to New Romney where they will be released by railway staff to find their way home in a race to Newcastle. Such trains were quite common in the fifties. The locomotive that day, 19 June 1959, was a fifty-one year old veteran Wainwright 'C' class No. 31588, which had been built at Ashford in 1908.

SOUTH EASTERN DIVISION • 19

Seen passing through the building site that was St Mary Cray Junction in April 1959 we see a long coal train from the Kent coalfield to one of the London power stations. What is interesting about the train is there are several different types of wagon being used to carry the coal. The motive power that day is provided by 'N' class No. 31408, at that stage allocated to Stewarts Lane shed.

May 1959 sees Standard Class 5, No. 73084 passing St Mary Cray Junction with a London to Ramsgate express. No. 73084, just under four years old at the time, was still allocated to her first shed at Stewarts Lane. The locomotive had been built at Derby in 1955 and was withdrawn in December 1965, a service life of only ten years. Briefly named *Tintagel*, the locomotive was always allocated to Southern Region at Stewarts Lane, Nine Elms and Feltham. This engine was scrapped in South Wales in 1966 like many Southern Region locomotives.

Above: A cold foggy morning on 4 March 1961 at St Mary Cray sees an unusual freight train heading east. The train, which had originated from Redbridge near Southampton the day before, was that morning running from Clapham Junction to Wrotham on the line between Swanley and Ashford. The special train is conveying new conductor rails for the Kent electrification scheme that was very much in full swing by early 1961. The motive power that day is also unusual and the train double-headed because of its weight and length. Class C No. 31317 is piloting unrebuilt 'Battle of Britain' No. 34067 *Tangmere*; the latter was always a distinctive loco because of its two nameplates (see picture at Knockholt). Also of note in this picture is the most unusual brake van.

Opposite above: December 1959 at St Mary Cray sees a London to Dover, via Maidstone, express bursting out under the footbridge from which Derek had taken several other pictures. The motive power that day is 'Schools' class, 30935 *Sevenoaks*. Withdrawn from Nine Elms shed at Christmas 1962, the locomotive was eventually cut up at the Cohens yard in July 1964. Such were the number of steam locomotives to be disposed of, many Southern Region locomotives were sent to distant scrapyards in South Wales, Norwich and, in this case, Kettering.

Opposite below: One of the now preserved 'Merchant Navy' class, No. 35028 *Clan Line*, at the time unrebuilt, is pictured at Petts Wood on a down boat train in April 1959. For a Stewarts Lane Bulleid pacific the engine is noticeably dirty. This locomotive has now spent many more years in preservation, as a rebuild, than working for British Railways. Thankfully it is a regular on the main line today and is always much cleaner! *Clan Line* is a fabulous and reliable locomotive and performs very well for a seventy-four year old.

SOUTH EASTERN DIVISION • 21

The down 'Golden Arrow' is pictured on the recently laid new formation near Petts Wood in July 1959. The train that day is hauled by unrebuilt 'Battle of Britain' class No. 34085 *501 Squadron*, which was at that time allocated to Stewarts Lane shed. Stewarts Lane had a number of Bulleid pacifics that were dedicated to these prestigious Pullman passenger services. These locomotives were always kept in both good mechanical condition and always very clean. Electrification is much in evidence here and once that had been completed, No. 34085 departed south London for Bournemouth shed in January 1961.

The first time the up 'Night Ferry' was hauled by an electric was 15 June 1959. Pictured at St Mary Cray we see 2,300hp electric locomotive No. E5003. Headcode 74 is 'Dover via Tonbridge and the Catford Loop'. The 'Night Ferry' had originated in Paris, hence the continental rolling stock, and travelled via the Dunkirk-Dover train ferry on to London as pictured here. Perhaps unusually for a first journey the electric was not carrying its newly designed 'Night Ferry' headboard.

SOUTH EASTERN DIVISION • 23

The first 'Merchant Navy' class, No. 35001 *Channel Packet*, is pictured passing Orpington in July 1959. Orpington is some fourteen miles from London and the start of three miles of 1 in 120 to the summit at Knockholt. The train is a down boat train to Folkestone Harbour. The Pacific will be detached at Folkestone Junction and tank engines attached to the rear of the train for the remainder of the journey to Folkestone Harbour. *Channel Packet* was built during the war (in 1941). It was rebuilt in August 1959, just a month after this photograph was taken, and withdrawn from service in November 1964.

BRCW delivered the first of what became the Class 33s to the Southern Region in January 1960. The type's first job was to replace steam on the South Eastern Division and here we see living proof as a three-month old No. D6505 passes through Chelsfield in July 1960, with a Charing Cross to Dover service. As diesels built in the early sixties go the Class 33s were very reliable, popular with train crews and long lasting, with four of the class main line registered today after sixty years of operation. No. D6505 itself did twenty-seven years in service before being scrapped at Vic Berry's yard in Leicester during October 1990. Many of the Class 33s were initially allocated to Hither Green depot in South London.

Above: A crisp October morning in 1959 sees a very clean, then fifty-seven years old, 'D1' class, No. 31739, passing through Chelsfield. The train has express passenger discs and Derek's notes show the service as 'down inspection saloon'. The platelayers on the left appear to be most disinterested as this Wainwright 4-4-0 of 1902 vintage passes them at speed. It has been suggested that the sloping Chelsfield Tunnel, just past Chelsfield railway station, was the inspiration for Edith Nesbit's popular children's classic *The Railway Children*.

Opposite above: The down 'Golden Arrow' is pictured climbing through Chelsfield station in September 1959. The train is hauled by Bulleid unrebuilt 'West Country' No. 34092 *City Of Wells*. At that stage the light pacific had been in service for ten years, having been built at Brighton in 1949. Later preserved, *City of Wells* has gone on to perform very well on many of the more steeply graded main lines in the north of England. No. 34092, and her sister No. 34107 were the two members of the 'West Country' class that changed their names. No. 34092 was initially named *Wells* and No. 34107 initially named *Blandford*, later becoming *Blandford Forum*.

Opposite below: When Derek returned from New Zealand, the family moved to Croydon in Surrey. Particular favourite places for him to go to take pictures were the adjacent stations of Chelsfield and Knockholt. These were an easy ten-mile journey along the A232 through West Wycombe. Pictured at Knockholt in September 1959 is the down 'Golden Arrow' hauled by rebuilt 'Merchant Navy' No. 35015 *Rotterdam Lloyd*.

SOUTH EASTERN DIVISION • 25

Most unusually for a Stewarts Lane Bullied pacific we see an absolutely filthy No. 34067, *Tangmere* passing through Knockholt with a down relief boat train to Folkestone. *Tangmere* was unique in the 'Battle of Britain' class because the locomotive carried two nameplates: the first, the name of the RAF airfield near Chichester that she had been named after and the second, a crest underneath the locomotive number on the side of the cab. This smaller crest says RAF Station Tangmere with 'Attack to Defend' written underneath. *Tangmere* was withdrawn from BR service very early from Salisbury shed in November 1963. The locomotive was preserved and has gone on to have a stellar career on the modern main line. The locomotive is presently being overhauled again.

Bursting out of Chelsfield Tunnel at Knockholt we see unrebuilt 'West Country' No. 34091 *Weymouth* heading south with a down boat train. There's a bit of a misconception that the lines from London through Kent were rather flat but the ruling gradient at this point on the line to the coast, just sixteen miles out of Charing Cross, is 1 in 120. The chalk cutting in the picture lets us know this is a picture in Kent but that aside the topography in this picture could be from much further north.

The 'Man of Kent' was a named express between Charing Cross and Margate that ran from 1953 to 1961. Usually named trains normally referred to a single service running each way; however, from 1956, there were two northbound and two southbound 'Man of Kent' services. The headboard we see here carries two shields: one depicts the White Horse of Kent and the other Invicta. Pictured passing through Knockholt in May 1960 with the up 'Man of Kent' to London is rebuilt 'West Country' pacific No. 34017 *Ilfracombe*.

Passing through Dunton Green station, two miles the London side of Sevenoaks, we see an electric test train in June 1959. Full-scale electrification came to this part of the Southern Region in 1961 and, in the eighteen months or so before that, special trains and crew training trips were more and more common. The train that day is hauled by No. E5001; this type of locomotive was later designated Class 71. This locomotive had been built in Doncaster and entered service in January 1959 so at this time it was only six months old. These locomotives were considered very successful, handling heavy boat trains as well as fitted freights. No. E5001 is now part of the National Collection and is presently being restored at its Shildon site in County Durham.

28 • THE DEREK CROSS COLLECTION: THE SOUTHERN IN TRANSITION 1946–1966

The 1.22pm push-pull service from Dunton Green to Westerham is pictured arriving at Westerham station on Tuesday 24 May 1960. Dominating the picture on the left hand side and watching over the goods yard is Westerham signal box. I have to say, as compared to some very attractive signal boxes we will see in this book, this one may not make the top ten! Everything is there: the fire buckets on the staircase, the name board, the signalman's bike at the bottom of the staircase and the chimney of the stove providing the heating … it just doesn't look very nice! Motive power that day was 'H' class No. 31520.

There were several routes out of London to the Kent coast: the main line through Orpington to Sevenoaks and the alternative route via Otford to Sevenoaks. Here, one morning in June 1959, we see a London to Folkestone Harbour boat train coming off the Otford via Bat & Ball line into Sevenoaks station. The locomotive that day is a very clean unrebuilt Bulleid pacific No. 34089 *602 Squadron*. The locomotive at that time was allocated to Stewarts Lane; it was rebuilt the following year and withdrawn in July 1967.

SOUTH EASTERN DIVISION • 29

Throughout the summer of 1959 one of the regular Bulleid unrebuilt pacifics on the prestige 'Golden Arrow' service was 'Battle of Britain' No. 34086 *219 Squadron*. Seen here in BR lined green livery the train is the 11am from London Victoria to Dover Marine and is pictured approaching Sevenoaks station. The photograph was taken on 3 July in that year. Steam continued to haul the 'Golden Arrow' for a further eleven months before giving way to BR-built electrics like No. E5001. No. 34086 remained in service until June 1966 before being scrapped in South Wales by Buttigiegs.

Emerging from the Sevenoaks Tunnel and approaching Weald signal box is Bulleid rebuilt 'West Country' class No. 34016 *Bodmin*. The train is an express from London to Ramsgate via Dover. The picture was taken in June 1960. *Bodmin* had been built at Brighton at the end of 1945, being rebuilt in 1958 and withdrawn in 1964. Operated by the Southern Railway and Southern Region for nineteen years between 1945 and 1964 *Bodmin* has been preserved and in private ownership for almost three times as long. A doughty main line performer for several years, the locomotive is not working presently but it was nice to see her and sister *Tangmere* coupled together and safely undercover at Carnforth in Lancashire in 2019.

Passing the Weald intermediate signal box we see Sulzer 1,160HP diesel No. D5014 on an up parcels train from Dover or Folkestone to London. No. D5014 had been built at Derby and, although nominally allocated to the London Midland Region, the locomotive was one of fifteen lent to the Southern Region in 1959 whilst the BRCW Type 3s were built. This locomotive had a working life of only sixteen years, being withdrawn in October 1975 from Eastfield depot in Glasgow. The locomotive, having worked on the LMR, SR and ScR was finally scrapped on the ER at Doncaster Works in March 1978.

Right at the tunnel mouth, at the south end of the nearly two-mile long Sevenoaks Tunnel we see 'H' class No. 31322 emerging into the daylight. The train is a Sevenoaks to Tonbridge local made up of some very vintage rolling stock as evidenced by the glimpse of the first vehicle of the train. No. 31322 had been built at Ashford in 1909 and remained in service from Tonbridge shed until January 1961. The picture was taken on 19 June 1959.

The down 'Golden Arrow' is pictured passing Weald Intermediate signal box in July 1960. The destination of the train that day is Dover, which was a recent change because for much of the fifties the southbound 'Golden Arrow' had travelled to Folkestone Harbour. The locomotive that day is a Bulleid 'Battle of Britain' class, No. 34086 *219 Squadron*, which she carries the full regalia of this prestigious named train. In France the train was known as the 'Fleche D'Or' and also carried locomotive headboards to that effect.

The 'Night Ferry' was, as the name suggests, a train that ran every night between London Victoria, Dover Marine, Dunkirk Maritime and Paris Nord. This was a train ferry service between London and Paris, which uniquely brought continental Wagons-Lits sleeping cars onto Britain's railway lines. These sleeping cars were modified to British loading gauge and were dedicated to this service, each set making three round trips a week. This rolling stock was also very heavy. Pictured at Weald in June 1959 we see the inward service from Paris on a summer's morning getting to grips with the 1 in 122 gradient towards Sevenoaks Tunnel. This train was often double headed and that morning some sixty-three years ago now the train engine is Bulleid 'West Country' No. 34093 *Saunton* piloted by 'L1' class No. 31789.

Above: Snow in Kent! Monday 11 January 1960 sees 'N' class No. 31856 passing Weald signal box with a northbound parcels and van train from Dover to London. The 'Ns' had been designed by Maunsell and this example had been built at Ashford in March 1925; it was one of a class of eighty locomotives, built in three batches, which were very reliable mixed traffic locomotives.

Opposite above: The 3.15pm Charing Cross to Deal service is seen close to Weald Intermediate signal box on the downhill section between Sevenoaks and Tonbridge. The next stop for this express would likely be Tonbridge, then Ashford and onwards towards the Kent coast. The picture was taken in September 1960. The locomotive, No. 30927 *Clifton*, was built in June 1934 and remained in service until early 1962, when it was withdrawn and scrapped in March that year.

Opposite below: The Allhallows branch ran from Gravesend to the early twentieth-century holiday resort of Allhallows-on-Sea on the River Thames, roughly opposite Southend-on-Sea. These two-coach trains shuttled between Gravesend and Allhallows and often crossed each other at Sharnal Street. The motive power that day was 'H' class No. 31517 propelling towards Allhallows and 'H' class, No.31512 waiting for the signal en route from Allhallows to Gravesend. Sixty years later the passenger service and the stations are long gone; however, modern intermodal container trains, steel trains and stone trains still run along the branch to the shipping terminal at Thamesport.

SOUTH EASTERN DIVISION • 33

The Allhallows branch from Stoke Junction, near Gravesend, was a late addition to the Southern Railway network. Built in 1932 the branch was made double track in 1935 and then singled again in 1957. This meant that trains often crossed at Sharnal Street and at Cliffe. In this picture, taken at Cliffe in March 1960, we see 'H' class No. 31512 propelling out of the station with a service from Gravesend to Allhallows, and the signalman returning to his signal box with a single line tablet. No. 31512, one of a class of sixty-six built to a design by Wainwright, was a regular on the branch and had been built at Ashford in 1909. On the front buffer beam there is a reference to regulator control, perhaps something to do with the push pull operation. The locomotive was withdrawn in June 1961. The branch passenger service ceased from 4 December 1961.

This picture neatly illustrates the vagaries of the Southern Railway/Southern Region locomotive numbering scheme. Pictured, we see No. 31512, an 'H' class tank engine built at Ashford in 1909, piloting a 'C' class tender engine, No. 31510, which was also built at Ashford but in 1904. Just to confirm the randomness of some of these numbers, the missing number, No. 31511, belonged to an 'E1', which had been built in 1905. Back to the picture we are on the Allhallows branch approaching Sharnal Street with the two locomotives hauling two elderly carriages on a service from Allhallows to Gravesend. The picture was taken in April 1960. This Kent side of the Thames estuary had a number of branches known as the 'Railways of Hoo'. Interestingly, as I write this in mid-2020, railways in this part of Kent are being looked at under 'restoring your railway' government scheme.

From time to time and reportedly especially at weekends, when trains were strengthened, the 'H' class monopoly on the branch was broken. Tender engines of Classes Q1 and C were often used and here we see 'C' class No. 31510 passing Grain Junction with a train from Gravesend to Allhallows. The picture was taken in April 1960. The branch onto the isthmus between the River Thames and the River Medway had nine stations and the area had in earlier times been a common holiday destination for Londoners.

A diverted boat train from London to Dover is pictured at the end of the fearsome climb from Maidstone East. Gradients of 1 in 60 are perhaps more associated with main lines further north but the route from Swanley through Maidstone to Ashford was severe and the steepest section was the three miles from the platform end at Maidstone East to Bearsted. The unrebuilt 'Battle of Britain' will be familiar as it is No. 34067 *Tangmere*; withdrawn in 1963 and subsequently preserved, it became a stalwart of the main line steam scene for many years. Currently at Carnforth being overhauled *Tangmere* was unusual as the locomotive had two nameplates as explained earlier in the book.

36 • THE DEREK CROSS COLLECTION: THE SOUTHERN IN TRANSITION 1946–1966

Opposite above: A more common order of the day was perhaps a named locomotive hauling an unnamed train. Here, however, in May 1950 we have the reverse. Pictured passing Teynham, between Sittingbourne and Faversham, we see 'Battle of Britain' class No. 34066, which was then unnamed, hauling the down 'Thanet Belle' between London Victoria and Margate. You will note the whole train comprises Pullman cars. This was a summer only train and only ran as a titled train between May 1948 and September 1950. Canterbury was added for summer 1951 and the name changed to the 'Kentish Belle'. One interesting point of this service, not recorded here, was that it also carried a 'Thanet Belle' tailboard.

Opposite below: When this photograph was taken in October 1950 British Railways was just over two years old, whilst 'D' class No. 31549 was forty-four. It is pictured departing from Canterbury West station with a stopping service from Margate to Ashford. The next station will be Chartham followed by Chilham, then Wye before reaching the final destination of Ashford. The Wainwright 'D' class eventually numbered fifty-one locomotives; these were nicknamed 'copper tops' because of their brightly coloured domes. They were very elegant locomotives – 'the epitome of solid Edwardian engineering'. They were also reliable performers that had put in some excellent work on boat trains between London and the Channel ports during the First World War.

Above: It is 3 July 1951 and 'D1' class No. 31145, allocated to Dover Marine, sits in Canterbury East station. The Pullman car train is a portion of the 'Kentish Belle', an all Pullman summer dated service, introduced between London Victoria and Ramsgate, which, for 1951 only, had a Canterbury portion. We think this is the second day of operation as this service, related to the Festival of Britain, only ran for the summer of 1951. The plan had been to start this service on 18 June 1951 but, for reasons not known, it was delayed until 2 July. The inclusion of Canterbury for the summer of 1951 caused the service to be renamed from the 'Thanet Belle' (Ramsgate only) to the 'Kentish Belle'. This new name was retained even after the Canterbury portion was dropped. The remaining service ran until 14 September 1958.

Pictured near Tilmanstone in April 1960 we see an early trial of a diesel shunter, No. D3044, which had been built at Derby in 1958, on coal traffic in the East Kent coalfield. In the foreground Stirling designed 'O1' class No. 31065, built at Ashford in 1896, awaits its next duty. Quite remarkably some sixty-two years after the picture was taken both these locomotives remain intact today. The diesel shunter, which later became No. 08032, worked for a long time in private industry for Foster Yeoman Ltd, and is now preserved on the Mid-Hants Railway. The 'O1', now 126 years old, is also preserved and has been a stalwart of the Bluebell Railway.

Maunsell 'U1' class No. 31904 is pictured passing through the Folkestone Warren with a cross-country service from Reading to Dover. Aside from the Tonbridge-allocated locomotive, which is filthy, the rolling stock, the permanent way and the recently installed fencing all look immaculate. The picture was taken at the end of May 1959.

SOUTH EASTERN DIVISION • 39

Snow, in the Folkestone Warren, is rare enough for me to include this picture of an empty stock train from Dover in January 1952. This ECS train is hauled by 'Scotch Arthur' No. 30779 *Sir Colgrevance*. Pictured at the western end of Folkestone Warren approaching the Martello tunnel, the train is still climbing, indeed the twelve miles from Dover to the summit near Sandling is uphill all the way. The train has just passed two signal cabins/halts at Abbotscliff and Warren Halt. These locations, because of the nature of the cliffs and the need for constant maintenance, were almost exclusively used for engineers and railway staff.

With Kearsney Junction signal box prominent in the foreground we see a double-headed coal train from the Kent coalfield approaching Dover. The train is the 1.40pm from Shepherds Well to Dover and is headed by two locally allocated locomotives: 'N' class No. 31818 tender-to-tender with 'O1' class No. 31258. The picture was taken on 2 May 1960.

Above: A Dover to London Victoria boat train, including a Pullman car as the third vehicle, is pictured at Folkestone Warren Halt in April 1950. The locomotive that day is a Maunsell 'King Arthur', one of the so-called 'Scotch Arthurs'; they had been given this nickname because they had been built by North British, in this case, in June 1925. The 'King Arthurs' built by North British had modified cabs to fit the eastern section loading gauge; they also had eight-wheel bogie tenders. No. 30776 was named *Sir Galagars*. A locomotive produced the same month in Glasgow, No. 30777 *Sir Lamiel*, is the only surviving member of the class that once numbered seventy-four locomotives. Folkestone Warren Halt at the foot of the white cliffs was mainly for railway staff use. Milepost 72 was on the platform.

Opposite above: Blue-liveried unrebuilt Bulleid 'Merchant Navy' class No. 35027 *Port Line* is pictured passing through the Folkestone Warren with the down 'Golden Arrow' in April 1950. For two years this 'Merchant Navy' had been allocated to Bournemouth shed but in 1950 was transferred to Stewarts Lane, returning to Bournemouth in 1955 and remaining there until withdrawal in 1966. Rebuilt in 1957, this locomotive has survived into preservation and is presently being restored at Eastleigh Works, where it had been built some seventy-four years ago now.

Opposite below: Halfway between Folkestone and Dover there was a small signal box at Abbotscliff. Pictured here, in the summer of 1959 with the white cliffs of Dover as a backdrop, we see unrebuilt Bulleid 'West Country' No. 34101 *Hartland* passing with a down relief boat train from London to Dover.

SOUTH EASTERN DIVISION • 41

The Maunsell 'W' class, built between 1932 and 1936 at Eastleigh and Ashford, comprised fifteen powerful freight tank engines. Many people said that they were basically a tank engine version of the 'N1'. They were also associated with transfer freights in the London area and also for a time served as banking engines at Exeter. So to see No. 31918, in the spring of 1951, heading east in the Folkestone Warren is rather rare. The train is an Ashford to Dover goods and, also rare, this locomotive spent its entire working life allocated to Norwood Junction shed from where it was withdrawn in August 1963; it was scrapped by February 1964.

Ambling through the Folkestone Warren in May 1952 we see two-year old Fairburn tank No. 42071, which had been built at Brighton in November 1950. The train is a stopper, all stations, from Shorncliffe to Ramsgate. No. 42071 spent ten years on the Southern Region before being transferred to Bletchley in December 1959 and was later allocated to Willesden, Oxley and Trafford Park before being withdrawn in March 1967.

SOUTH EASTERN DIVISION • 43

This May 1952 view sees an up van train passing through the Folkestone Warren. What made this such a favourite for Derek was the fact that the railway ran along the 'White Cliffs of Dover' for two or three miles between the Martello Tunnel, just east of Folkestone to the Shakespeare Cliff Tunnel, a mile west of Dover Marine. This piece of railway was limited to 60 mph, reportedly because of the risk of rock fall. The penultimate vehicle on this train is of interest because it is a gas tank on a railway wagon. The locomotive that day was N class, No. 31865.

The spring of 1951 sees 'L1' class No. 31783 passing through the Folkestone Warren in a westerly direction. The train is interesting for all sorts of reasons; it is an inter-regional service from Deal to Birkenhead, it only has two coaches and the coaches are of Great Western Railway origin. The coaches also carry destination boards. This service was one that picked up different portions along the way so that by the time it got to Birkenhead it probably had eight to ten coaches. Also of note in this picture, and with others in the book taken during this period, is the absolutely pristine permanent way. These inter-regional trains had begun as far back as 1904 when LNWR inaugurated 'the Sunny South special' from stations in the midlands to Eastbourne and Brighton. Two world wars stopped these trains but they resumed in 1949 and their importance grew with long-distance holidays and cross-Channel travel becoming more popular.

44 • THE DEREK CROSS COLLECTION: THE SOUTHERN IN TRANSITION 1946–1966

A mid-Winter picture in January 1952 has seen snow the night before give way to a fine, cold morning at Folkestone Junction. Folkestone Junction, some seventy-one miles from London and six miles from Dover Marine, was where the branch to Folkestone Harbour left the main line. There were also substantial sidings here at this time. A Maidstone to Dover local is pictured setting off on the last leg of the journey behind 'L' class No. 31761. A Beyer Peacock loco of 1914, this locomotive and No. 31769 were the first two of the class of twenty-two to be withdrawn in 1956.

The empty stock of the 'Golden Arrow' is pulled out of the Harbour station by double-headed GWR Panniers Nos. 4601 and 4616, with smoke at the rear of the train indicating a banker as well. The picture, taken in May 1959, shows the empty stock going back to Folkestone Junction to be prepared for the journey back to London later the same day. These two tanks had both migrated from South Wales – Abercynon and Barry respectively – and would remain in service until November 1962 and October 1964. No. 4616 had by then returned to Wales and was withdrawn from Pontypool Road.

An up boat train, having connected with a cross-Channel ferry, is pictured setting off on the seventy-two mile journey to London Victoria. A standing start, a long train and tight curves would be hard work for the pair of Panniers. A Pullman car for First Class lunches is included in the train formation. Although the branch was only a mile long, it was very busy at this time and as you can see in the distance was fully signalled. The train is headed by Pannier tanks Nos. 4616 and 4692. Also of note in this picture is the main road, the A260 Tram Road, and emerging from London Street is, I think, a Vauxhall Velox. Equally of note is the total absence of any other cars in this town centre street … but it was July 1959!

Emerging from the instantly recognisable Shakespeare Cliff Tunnel, a mile west of Dover Marine station, is a London to Margate service in June 1950. The locomotive is 'Schools' class No. 30908 *Westminster*. Of interest, in equal measure in this picture, are the very varied passenger rolling stock on the train and the very varied open wagons in the foreground on a head shunt from Dover Western Docks.

Above: The circumstances of this combination on the down 'Golden Arrow', pictured near Shorncliffe in June 1951, are not clear! I think even if they were clear British Railways Southern Region may not want to have admitted the reasons for this double-header. Pictured in the same month as No. 70014 *Iron Duke* was put into service, the 'Golden Arrow' is being piloted by 'Schools' class No. 30903 *Charterhouse*. We think that the 'Britannia' class had probably failed en route to Dover and the 'Schools' class, locally allocated to St Leonards in Hastings, had been summoned to the rescue and take the prestigious named train the final eight miles to Dover Marine.

Opposite above: I'm not sure how many stations in the British Isles have had three different names. At the time Derek took this picture the station behind the train was known as Shorncliffe. When the station originally opened to serve an army camp it was known as Shorncliffe Camp, changing its name to Shorncliffe in the mid-twenties and to Folkestone West in 1962. The train is also interesting, being hauled by one of the German (Borsig) 'L' class – No. 31775. The locomotive has joined BR, while the tender retains its Southern Railway markings. The train is a local service from Shorncliffe to Ramsgate and appears to have left a van in the platform, which the 'R1' class in the distance may be off to collect. The picture was taken in June 1950.

Opposite below: An up continental van train with both French and British rolling stock is pictured passing through Shorncliffe station on an April day in 1951. The train is hauled by 'Schools' class No. 30920 *Rugby*. The locomotive, after some years at Bricklayers Arms shed, had recently been re-allocated to Ramsgate, where it remained for much of the fifties, before withdrawal from Brighton shed in November 1961.

SOUTH EASTERN DIVISION • 47

This April 1950 picture depicts another virtually new locomotive passing Saltwood with an up train from Margate to London. 'Battle of Britain' No. 34089 in unbranded malachite green livery had been built at Brighton in December 1948 and was just sixteen months old when the picture was taken. The locomotive was later named *602 Squadron* and remained in service, latterly in rebuilt form, until the end of Southern Region steam in July 1967.

Pictured in May 1951, an early morning service from Maidstone to Dover is pictured on the down gradient at Saltwood between Sandling Junction and Folkestone West. From Folkestone West the train will continue through the Folkestone Warren to Dover, about eleven miles away from where the picture was taken. The locomotive that day was 'L' class No. 31762; also of interest, the parcel vans at the back of the train appear to outnumber the passenger coaches.

SOUTH EASTERN DIVISION • 49

A little more than two years old we see Bulleid 'Merchant Navy' No. 35029 *Ellerman Lines* in blue livery passing Saltwood in March 1951. Saltwood was just east of Sandling station, the junction for the branch line to Hythe, and ten miles from Dover Priory, where this train had begun its journey to London. *Ellerman Lines*, the penultimate 'Merchant Navy' to be built at Eastleigh in 1949, was like all the thirty strong class, rebuilt in the late fifties. No. 35029 was withdrawn from Weymouth shed in 1966 and actually only after withdrawal did the locomotive become more famous. After nearly a decade at the famous Barry scrapyard of Woodham Bros, the locomotive was secured for the National Collection and transferred to York when it was sectioned (cut vertically down the middle) to show future generations how a steam engine worked. The locomotive remains at York today in rebuilt form and in BR green livery.

The 'J' class was Wainwright's last design for the South Eastern & Chatham Railway; it was a bigger version of the most successful 'H' class. Built for heavy outer-suburban work, this unusual 0-6-4T class comprised only five locomotives. All were built at Ashford in 1913 and all were allocated to that shed for many years. All five examples made it to British Railways days (as written on the side tanks here) and all were renumbered in 1948/1949. No. 31599 was the first to be withdrawn at the end of 1949 and the other four members of the class succumbed over the next two years. Pictured here at Saltwood in March 1950 the first of the class, No. 31595, is on a Dover to Maidstone stopping service.

Above: Just two months old in May 1951, immaculate Crewe-built 'Britannia' No. 70004 *William Shakespeare* is seen passing through Sandling Junction with the down 'Golden Arrow' to Dover. Sandling was the junction for the branch to Hythe and on the left of the picture we see the Hythe branch platform. The two 'Britannias', No. 70004 and her sister No. 70014 *Iron Duke*, were allocated to Stewarts Lane shed to work the prestigious 'Golden Arrow' boat trains. Both locomotives were transferred away to the LMR at Trafford Park shed in June 1958.

Opposite above: A bright moody morning in March 1950 sees blue liveried Bulleid 'Merchant Navy' class No. 35026 passing Ashford West with an up boat train to London. No. 35026 had been built at Eastleigh in December 1948 and would later be named 'Lamport & Holt Line'. As we can see the locomotive, although carrying nameplates, has them covered over. The whole class was named after famous shipping lines but, until the locomotive had been named officially, the nameplates remained covered up. In the case of No. 35026 and the now preserved No. 35028 *Clan Line*, both were named on the same day, 15 January 1951. Also of interest is the fact that No. 35026 was put to service in December 1948 in malachite green, repainted blue in July 1949 and further repainted into BR green in June 1952, so three liveries in less than four years.

Opposite below: This March 1951 picture passing the allotments alongside Ashford West Junction shows an 'N' class and Fairburn tank back-to-back, double-heading a service from Ashford to Maidstone. At that time this unusual combination was a regular on this turn and we think this was used as a means of getting a locomotive moved from Ashford to Maidstone. The train engine is Fairburn No. 42072, built only five months earlier at Brighton and, although first allocated to Stewarts Lane shed, the locomotive almost at once moved to Ashford shed. No. 42072 would be withdrawn from Low Moor shed near Bradford just sixteen years later, having been allocated to ten sheds in its short active service life! The pilot engine that day, 'N' class No. 31810, was the first of the class dating back to June 1917. This was Maunsell's first design since taking over from Wainwright in 1913. Eventually eighty-one 'Ns' were built and a first class, reliable, mixed traffic engine resulted.

SOUTH EASTERN DIVISION • 51

52 • THE DEREK CROSS COLLECTION: THE SOUTHERN IN TRANSITION 1946–1966

This April 1950 picture at Ashford sees another double-headed service about to set off, this time on a stopping passenger: the 10.48am to New Romney via Lydd. The motive power that day is 'H' class No. 31327 piloting 'L1' class No. 31757. The second station on this leisurely journey will be Appledore, where the lines to Hastings and New Romney diverged. The 'L1' was later to become well-known, to a number of railway modellers, as the Tri-ang OO gauge example carried the number 31757. The branch remains open today for occasional freight trains serving the nuclear power plant at Dungeness.

With goods or parcel carrying vehicles again outnumbering passenger coaches by two to one we see 0-6-4T 'J' class No. 31598 between Ashford and Sevington. This 'mixed train' is a stopping service from Ashford to Dover. The picture was taken in November 1949. Only five 'J' class were built, all in 1913, and all made it through to the advent of British Railways Southern Region in 1948 … but not much longer!

SOUTH EASTERN DIVISION • 53

A beautiful picture of an ancient 'E' class 4-4-0 busy shunting empty stock (for a service to Margate) at Ashford in May 1951, some seventy-one years ago now. No. 31514 had been built at Ashford works in April 1907 and was withdrawn in December 1951 from Ashford shed after forty-four years' service to the South Eastern & Chatham Railway, Southern Railway and Southern Region of British Railways. Although BR had been in operation for more than three years this locomotive, aside from its numbers, shows no British Railways branding. The Wainwright designed 'Es' were a development of the 'D' class and were fitted with the large Belpaire firebox. Twenty-six 'Es' were built, eleven of which were converted to 'E1s'.

Saturday 10 June 1961 was the last day steam operated on the South Eastern Division before electrification took over the bulk of the workings the following Monday. In this quite remarkable picture we see 'D1' class No. 31739, which had been built at Ashford in 1902, still active on passenger work, arriving at Ashford. The train is the 4.12pm Tonbridge to Ashford local.

July 1951 sees almost new 'Britannia' pacific No. 70014 *Iron Duke* accelerating away from Ashford with the down boat train for Dover. The passenger rolling stock on the train is very varied but slightly upstaged by a row of ancient cattle wagons on the right-hand side. We believe these wooden-bodied vehicles to be from the late 1890s and of Midland Railway origin. The two 'Britannias', *Iron Duke* and *William Shakespeare*, were both allocated to Nine Elms shed (70A) from new and, although it is often said they were the only 'Britannias' allocated to the Southern Region, this is not true as in 1953 other members of the class were allocated to Exmouth Junction, Salisbury and Stewarts Lane to cover when the Bulleid pacifics were being examined and repaired after an axle incident at Crewkerne. It is of note that the two locomotives sent new to the Southern Region lasted in service until almost the end of steam on BR, both being withdrawn from Carlisle Kingmoor shed in December 1967.

Remarkably clean but without any BR crest 'J' class No. 31596 is pictured accelerating away from Ashford with a stopping service to Maidstone. The smoke effect and the lifting safety valves suggest the train crew were in a hurry to get the nineteen-mile journey completed in good time. The picture was taken in March 1950 and No. 31596, with its unusual 0-6-4T wheel arrangement for a class in the UK, remained in service until October 1951, achieving just under forty years of service.

A wet February day in 1951 sees 'WD' 2-8-0 No. 90226 passing through Wye station with an eastbound oil special. These locomotives were rare on the Southern Region and only operated for two or three years after nationalisation before being transferred to the north. No. 90226 was allocated to Bricklayers Arms at this time but transferred to Manchester Newton Heath later in 1951.

Another beautiful picture taken on a sunny March day in 1951, sees Wainwright 'D' class No. 31549 on the daily pick-up goods between Minster and Ashford. Fifty-one 'Ds' were built between 1901 and 1907 at five different sites: Ashford, Dübs & Co, Vulcan Foundry, Sharp Stewart and Robert Stephenson. The class was recognised as being one of the most elegant locomotive designs of the period. The locomotive is in BR livery but the tender appears to have missed out on a crest. Sister locomotive No. 31737 is preserved as part of the National Collection and is presently in York Museum. No. 31737 reportedly ran 1.7 million miles, rather proving the point that these locomotives both performed well and were reliable. This is an average of 13,000 miles a year, every year, from 1901 to 1956.

Unrebuilt and unnamed Bulleid light pacific No. 34086 is seen pulling away from the Wye stop on a stopping train from Margate to Ashford. New to Ramsgate shed in 1948 No. 34086 is in blue BR livery. Many of the Bulleid light pacifics were named after the individuals and RAF Squadrons that had played a key part in the Battle of Britain and were later known as the 'Battle of Britain' class. This locomotive was later named *219 Squadron* and became a regular, in BR green livery, on the 'Golden Arrow' in the late fifties. Later transferred to Exmouth Junction the locomotive was withdrawn in June 1966.

One of the benefits of taking pictures at Wye was that, from time to time, locomotives overhauled at Ashford works might appear on running-in turns. On a glorious day in June 1951, Beyer Peacock-built 'L' class, No. 31760 is pictured on the Minster to Ashford pick-up goods. The locomotive is looking pristine and would remain in service for another ten years before being withdrawn from Nine Elms shed in London in June 1961.

SOUTH EASTERN DIVISION • 57

Pictured leaving Wye, on a dull day in April 1952, we see Wainwright 'E' class No. 31166 with a stopping train from Ramsgate to Ashford. The 'E' class was closely related to the 'D' class but with a Belpaire boiler and a longer smokebox. They were more powerful than the 'D' class and eleven of the original twenty-six locomotives were later rebuilt by Maunsell as 'E1s'. This example – No. 31166 still without a BR smokebox numberplate – was the last to be withdrawn in May 1955.

This June 1950 picture, near Wye, shows Wainwright 'C' class No. 1260 with a pick-up goods from Minster to Ashford; this was a distance of just under twenty-seven miles. A total of 109 of the class were built between 1900 and 1908 and they were capable of hard work over the whole SECR network. This example, as well as having what appears to be the tender of another locomotive, displays the transition from Southern Railway to Southern Region. Officially renumbered in August 1950 to its BR number of 31260, it appears to have been half done two months earlier in June. British Railways appears on the tender with no crest and the Southern Railway number 1260 appears on the locomotive with a small letter 's' in front. It has neither a BR front numberplate nor a shedplate. In May 1953 No 31260 was one of the first of the class to be withdrawn.

Rolling into the station stop at Wye, in March 1952, we see 'Schools' class No. 30915, *Brighton* with a through service along the south coast from Ramsgate to Hastings. The lone passenger waits to join the train but appears to be taking no interest in either the 1933-built Maunsell locomotive or Derek Cross, the photographer. No. 30915, at that stage, was allocated to Ramsgate shed and was in service from 1933 to 1962.

On a wet day in March 1952 we see a pair of 'N' class locomotives passing through the station at Wye with a long coal train, in mainly wooden bodied wagons, from Chislet to Battersea. Chislet Colliery, two miles east of Sturry, was one of a number of collieries in the then extensive Kent coalfield on this railway line between Minster and Ashford. The Maunsell-designed 'N' class were built in several batches, all at Ashford, and here we see No. 31819, built in 1922, piloting No. 31404, built in 1932. No. 31404, the newer of the pair, has a larger 4,000 gallon tender.

SOUTH EASTERN DIVISION • 59

Setting off from Wye station past the signal box we see 'D' class No. 31549 with a stopping service along the Stour Valley from Ashford to Ramsgate. No. 31549 had been built at Ashford in September 1906 and remained in service for fifty years until being withdrawn in 1956. It was one of the last four members of the 'D' class in service and was, by that time, based at Guildford shed.

As mentioned in the introduction Derek attended Wye College and it seems in this picture, taken in June 1951, a couple of his student friends have boarded the service from Ramsgate to Ashford and are looking at him. Wye is the last stop on this journey and Ashford, five miles away, probably a quarter of an hour distant. I'm absolutely certain his student friends did not appreciate the quite wonderful birdcage coaches they were travelling in. Motor power that day is 'H' class No. 31519 in full British Railways livery but the old Southern Railway number still evident on the front buffer beam.

We've commented before in this book about how important rural railways were until the mid-twentieth century. The Hawkhurst branch saw a regular two-coach passenger service but it also had a daily freight service along its length. Pictured at Goudhurst, in March 1960, is filthy 'C' class No. 31590 setting off from the station towards Paddock Wood. The loading siding in the foreground has bright rails and perhaps one of the wagons, now on the train, has been recovered from that siding and is now going back empty to Paddock Wood. In earlier days the Hawkhurst branch was famous for conveying local potatoes and pot plants to the markets in London.

Cranbrook in Kent was the closest station to the well-known girl's boarding school at Benenden. Six times a year, at the beginning and end of the three terms, a school special was run from London's Charing Cross station to Cranbrook to accommodate the children travelling to and from the school. For the start of the summer term in 1960 'D1' class No. 31749 is seen pulling away from Cranbrook station with the school special. In the background a single-deck bus is evident as is the most enormous station house.

The Hawkhurst branch left the main line at Paddock Wood and wandered through the fields and orchards for eleven miles or so to Hawkhurst. Derek felt a journey on this rural branch line was everyone's idea of the County of Kent at its best! He thought the branch epitomised the (now) lost charm of post-war rural railways. This picture was taken at Horsmonden station with typical oast houses as the backdrop on a May morning in 1960. The train is the first of the day from Paddock Wood to Hawkhurst and is hauled by an 'H' class (of 1909 vintage), No. 31193. The locomotive, allocated to Tonbridge shed, had less than a year left in service, being withdrawn in March 1961. One of the train crew appears to be keeping a watchful eye on Derek! The branch to Hawkhurst closed on 12 June 1961.

This March 1960 picture is at Goudhurst, a wayside station on the Hawkhurst branch. Hawkhurst is a village in the attractive High Weald area of Kent and in the sixties was linked to the main line on a branch line to Paddock Wood. This branch line, built in 1892, had three wayside stations, including Goudhurst. The motive power that day is 'H' class No. 31177, which had been built at Ashford in 1909 and which was allocated to Tonbridge shed at the time the photograph was taken.

62 • THE DEREK CROSS COLLECTION: THE SOUTHERN IN TRANSITION 1946–1966

Derek's notes on the back of his print say 'big day for the Hawkhurst branch' I think that by this he means the normal auto-train service and daily freight have been supplemented by the school special for Benenden School. He records the train as being the 2.46pm Charing Cross to Cranbrook and it is pictured passing through Goudhurst behind 'D1' No. 31749. He also makes mention of the very ornate station lamps. The picture was taken on Tuesday 3 May 1960.

Rush hour at Hawkhurst! Pictured at Hawkhurst in July 1960 we see 'H' class No. 31533 clearing the platform with some empty coaches. The Hawkhurst branch saw special school trains six times a year and this day at the end of the summer term has seen the need to hide other passenger stock in the goods shed. The train in the goods shed that day is headed by 'C' class No. 31592 (which was later preserved). The branch had been opened in 1892 and engineered by the famous Colonel Stephens, who later built the Kent & East Sussex Railway.

SOUTH EASTERN DIVISION • 63

Right up to the end of steam in 1961 a feature of the workings in Kent was the fairly indiscriminate use of what motive power they had on very different trains. Hop pickers' specials tended to attract whatever locomotives were available and here we see 'C' class, No. 31693 restarting such a service from Wateringbury, the neo-Gothic station on the line from Paddock Wood to Maidstone West: the Medway Valley branch. No. 31693 was built in 1900 by Neilson Reid in Scotland and here she was sixty years later working a passenger train. The picture was taken on 18 September 1960.

It's always good to see a locomotive, which we have enjoyed now for over fifty-five years in preservation, at work before it was preserved. Pictured here is Wainwright 'H' class No. 31263 of 1905 vintage in her BR days arriving at Yalding. The train is a Maidstone West to Ashford for onward connection to Tonbridge. The locomotive has spent most of its preserved life on the Bluebell Railway and is presently in SECR green livery as number 263.

Above: The last day of the Hawkshurst branch was 11 June 1961; this was also the last day of the surviving freight only section of the Kent & East Sussex Railway between Robertsbridge and Tenterden and so a rail tour was organised! For this section two 'Terriers' were provided, one at each end of the train, or top and tail in modern language. Pictured at Northiam No. 32662, formally *Martello*, leads the train with No. 32670 at the rear. The latter was the former KESR No. 3 *Bodiam*, which appropriately led the return train and the final working on the branch. This last day was also the first day a Pullman car made it to Tenterden.

Opposite above: The 'Golden Arrow' from London Victoria to Dover was the prestige service to France. The Channel was crossed by ferry and the French equivalent, 'La Fleche D'Or', carried the passengers to Paris. By 1960 the all-Pullman formation had given way to Pullmans and day coaches. Competition from air travel was beginning to emerge. The train is hauled by rebuilt 'Battle of Britain' class No. 34088 *213 Squadron*, a regular on this train and a Stewarts Lane favourite. An interesting point, in passing, about Paddock Wood station was that it was unique in that on the down platform there was an office labelled 'Hop Control' in big letters. It was from this office that the special hop picking trains and additional trains at the weekends for the 'hop-pickers' friends' trains', for those coming to visit the families, were co-ordinated.

Opposite below: One of the reasons Derek spent so much time in and around Paddock Wood was, we think, because of the great variety of motive power that was evident there is the late fifties and early sixties. There were the boat trains to Dover and Folkestone, the endless freight traffic as well as the local branch line services. Pictured here is a service from Maidstone West to Tonbridge and on this occasion, on 10 June 1961, Bulleid 'Q1' class No. 33031 provides the motive power. One of the early withdrawals in September 1963 from Three Bridges shed (75E) No. 33031 had a working life of twenty-one years.

SOUTH EASTERN DIVISION • 65

With an enormously long freight train of over fifty wagons, 'Q1' class No. 33034 comes off the Maidstone West line and into Ashford station. It is thought the destination of this very mixed freight was probably the large marshalling yard at Tonbridge. The whole picture is about freight and the varied nature of the wagon types in the yard on the left adds to the considerable interest of the picture. No. 33034 had been built at Ashford in 1942 and was at that time a Tonbridge engine, later transferring to Guildford where it was withdrawn in early 1964.

The electrification of the Kent coast is very much underway and almost complete in this June 1961 photograph at Paddock Wood. As well as the third rail everywhere there are at least three sets of brand new electric multiple-units in the sidings on the downside of the station. We suppose in connection with the electrification a lot of train crew had to be trained and here we see a driver training special being propelled through the station on the fast line towards Ashford by Standard tank No. 80037. What is very interesting is the single coach being used for the training; we think it's an SECR inspection saloon. No. 80037 had been new to Watford shed in May 1952, later transferred to three Southern Region sheds before going to the S&D where it was involved on the final passenger services on the line between Bath and Bournemouth.

The down 'Golden Arrow' again is pictured passing through Paddock Wood station at speed behind unrebuilt 'Battle of Britain' class No. 34086 *219 Squadron*. Paddock Wood is thirty-five miles from London, just under half way to Dover Marine, some seventy-seven miles from London. That day in June 1960 the train was in fact running to Dover; for a long period before that the southbound 'Golden Arrow' had used Folkestone Harbour instead.

Pictured passing the distinctive signal box at Paddock Wood, one afternoon in June 1960, we see a Ramsgate via Dover to London service slowing for the station stop. The train is hauled by a Maunsell 'Schools' class No. 30931 *King's Wimbledon*. No. 30931 had been built in 1934 at Eastleigh and was withdrawn as a result of the Kent coast electrification just over a year later in September 1961.

68 • THE DEREK CROSS COLLECTION: THE SOUTHERN IN TRANSITION 1946–1966

Just out of Tonbridge on a 1 in 47 gradient we see a 'D1' class climbing past Somerhill Tunnel towards High Brooms and Tunbridge Wells. The train is a Tonbridge to Hastings service. The train that day in May 1960 is hauled by No. 31735, which had been built back in 1901 by Sharp Stewart. The locomotive remained in service for just a few more months, being withdrawn in April the following year, from Eastleigh shed (71A).

Unusually, the goods yard at the west end of Tonbridge station is still today in use for freight traffic by GBRf. The motive power in those days seventy-one years ago was, however, substantially different and here we see departing from the goods yard with a long transfer freight 'Schools' class No. 30906 *Sherborne*, at that stage allocated to St Leonards shed in Hastings. The picture was taken in October 1951.

SOUTH EASTERN DIVISION • 69

All the evidence in this photograph, including the ex-SECR Birdcage set, indicates that it was taken in 1950 just after Nationalisation two years earlier. Further evidence of this is the very clean panel underneath the fireman's window where the number 31727 is written in new paint. This suggests this 'D1' class had just been given its British Railways number. A further interesting aspect to the photograph is the proliferation of wires and telegraph poles that dominate the left-hand side of the picture. Not uncommon in those days, such wires are rarely seen today.

October 1950 sees 'L1' No. 31758 heading west on the line to Redhill with a local train from Tonbridge to Redhill. On the left of the picture the main line to London, twenty-nine miles away, can be seen at the start of the climb towards Hildenborough. On the right of the picture an unidentified 'R1' class can be seen taking a break between shunting duties. On the left of the picture behind the signal box there is a white building, which I'm given to understand was one of only a small number in England, as it was a cricket ball factory.

Passing Penshurst station some four miles west of Tonbridge on the line to Redhill we see a Saturday summer dated train from Margate to Birkenhead. Hauling the train, that day in May 1960, is a pair of diesel locomotives, both just over a year old. The first locomotive, No. D5000, had been built at Derby in July 1958. These new 1,160hp diesel locomotives were part of the 1955 Modernisation Plan. Initially allocated to the Midland, Eastern and Scottish regions, fifteen of the LMR allocation were transferred to the Southern Region between 1959 and 1962, whilst construction of the BRCW Type 3s (later Class 33) took place. Pictured here is No. D5009 piloting No. D5012; the two engines remained in service until 1976 and 1975 respectively and both were later scrapped at Doncaster Works.

A very striking picture of a Wainwright 'L' class at Penshurst in the summer of 1959. Derek records this picture as having been taken in July of that year and this may have been one of the No. 31778's last journeys as records show that the locomotive was withdrawn and scrapped by the end of August 1959. The train is a stopping service from Tonbridge to Redhill, a distance of just under twenty miles. The next stop after Penshurst will be Edenbridge.

Winter of 1960 sees a westbound goods passing through Penshurst at the start of a ten-mile climb towards the North Downs through stations at Edenbridge and Godstone, before reaching the summit at Bletchingley tunnel. The locomotive is a Maunsell 'N1', No. 31879. This class was effectively a three-cylinder version of the 'N' class and had been built with work over the Tonbridge to Hastings route over which the two-cylinder 'Ns' could not work because of restricted clearances. This line between Tonbridge and Redhill was well aligned and often saw some high speed running.

January 1960 sees the diverted 'Golden Arrow' express racing through Penshurst station towards Tonbridge and its final destination of Dover. We suspect the train was diverted via Redhill to Tonbridge because of electrification of the more direct mainline from Victoria. The locomotive complete with headboard and flags is unrebuilt 'Battle of Britain' class No. 34085 *501 Squadron*. This Bulleid pacific was rebuilt six months later and remained in service until September 1965, a working life of just seventeen years.

The wayside station at Penshurst would seem to me to be a bit of a modeller's dream! In this picture we can see a tunnel, a loading gauge, a small goods yard, a station with staggered platforms, semaphore signals and all overlooked by the rather attractive church of St John the Baptist. The locomotive that day, on a local bound for Redhill, was Maunsell 'U1' class No. 31902.

Edenbridge High Level, on the line from Tonbridge to Redhill, was called that in order to differentiate it from Edenbridge Town, which was on the line from Hurst Green Junction towards Eridge and Uckfield. Here we see an engineer's ballast train on the High Level line crossing over the Edenbridge Town line. The train is hauled by a 'back to back' combination of 'C' class No. 31724 and 'U1' class No. 31898. The picture was taken in June 1960.

The business end of the weed killer. Pictured here near Edenbridge High Level is a weed killing special, going away from the camera, heading for Lewes and hauled by 'K' class No. 32347. In the foreground we see a twin set of converted PMVs (Nos. DS469 and DS466) both spraying the track and from where the management of the train was located. The picture is dated mid-June 1959.

March 1960 again sees 'D1' class No. 31735 in the platform at Edenbridge High Level. The train is a stopper from Redhill to Tonbridge; the next stop will be Penshurst. The train engine that day is 'D1' No. 31735, which was of November 1901 vintage. The 'D1s' were built by five different companies. This example was built by Sharp Stewart in Glasgow. No. 31735 remained in service until April 1961 and was, interestingly, allocated to nine different sheds between the start of British Railways Southern Region in 1948 and the locomotive's withdrawal in 1961.

The doyen of the Maunsell 'Schools' class was No. 900 *Eton*, built in March 1930, and for many years allocated to St Leonards. It had, by the time this picture was taken in March 1960, been transferred to Brighton shed, 75A, as the shed plate shows. The picture was taken at Edenbridge High Level on the line between Redhill and Tonbridge and is of an eastbound freight, with Tonbridge the likely destination. 'Schools' class locomotives on freight were not common.

Betchworth in March 1960 and a very mixed eastbound freight is pictured passing through the station. Waiting at the level crossing we see a 1960s St Ivel delivery truck; in those days over sixty years ago it was very striking in its distinctive livery. The locomotive – 'S15' No. 30836 – was built in 1927 to Maunsell's design; this was a development of Urie's original design with higher boiler pressure, reduced diameter cylinders and modified cabs. No. 30836 was also one of five locomotives fitted with smaller tenders for working on the central section.

SOUTH EASTERN DIVISION • 75

A very long eastbound goods train is pictured climbing through Betchworth station on a 1 in 196 gradient. Derek records the train as being an inter-regional freight between Tonbridge and Reading via Redhill. The line from Redhill to Reading is some forty-six miles in length and Betchworth some five miles into the journey. The locomotive that day in May 1960 is 'N' class No. 31865, which had been built at Ashford thirty-five years earlier in 1925.

This March 1960 picture at Betchworth sees a Dover to Reading train pulling away from the station. The next stop will be Dorking Town. The locomotive is GWR Mogul No. 6385, which had been built by Robert Stephenson & Company in 1921. The locomotive at that time was allocated to Reading shed and was withdrawn from Didcot shed in November 1963.

SOUTH CENTRAL DIVISION

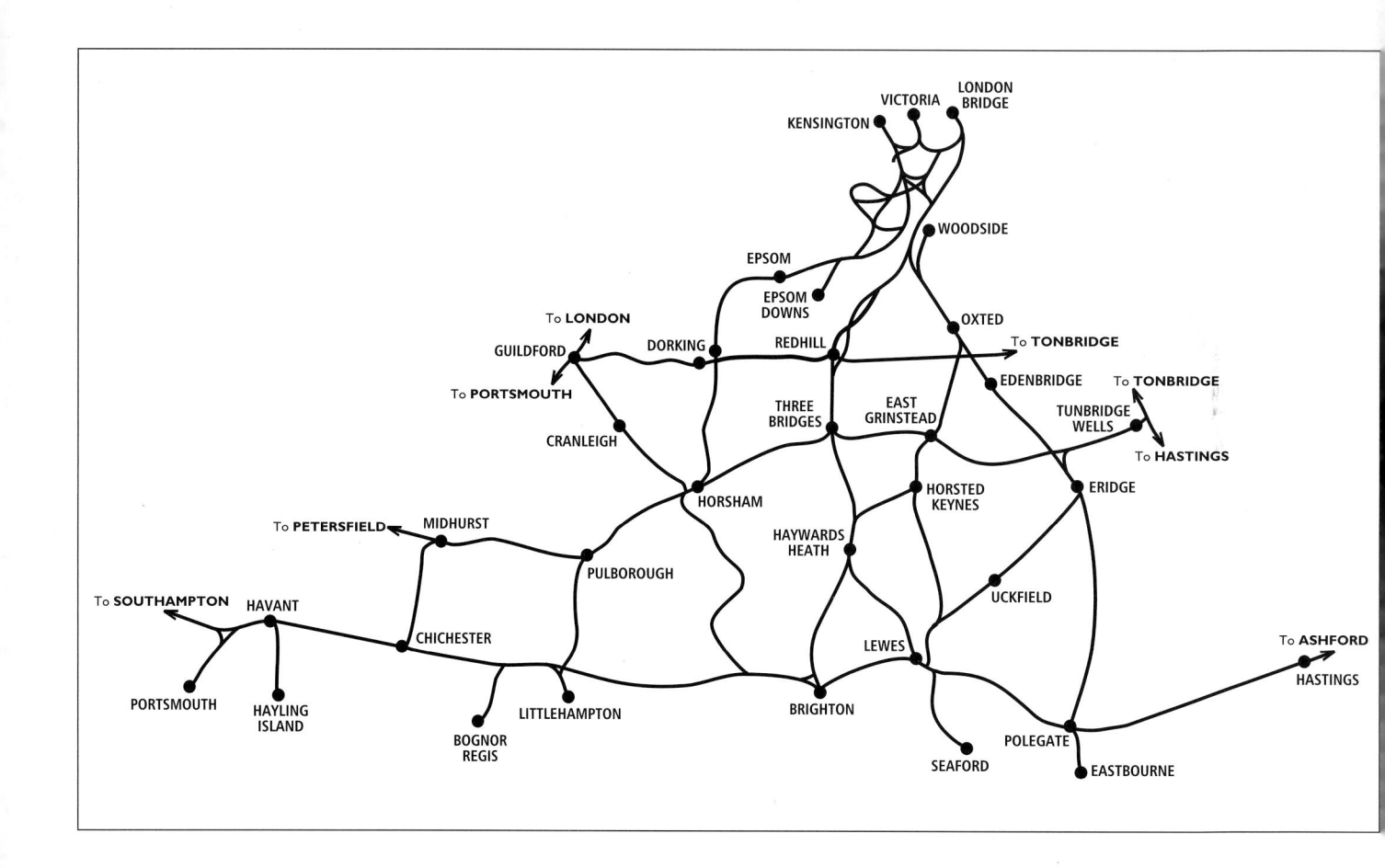

Opposite above: Spring of 1960 sees Maunsell 'Schools' class No. 30906 *Sherborne* leaving Dorking Town with a train from Reading to Redhill. *Sherborne* was one of forty 'Schools' class built between 1930 and 1935; the type was the last design of 4-4-0 locomotive to appear in this country. They performed all over the Southern Region with great success and Harold Holcroft, the technical assistant to Maunsell, the CME of the Southern Railway, was of the opinion that the 'Schools' were 'the best value for money ever put on rails'.

Opposite below: Pictured storming away from the stop and past the signal box at Dorking Town is Churchward-designed GWR Mogul No. 7331. The train is a Dover to Reading service and that day has a uniform rake of modern Mk.1 coaches. No. 7331 had been built in 1932 at Swindon as No. 9309 and had been renumbered in May 1959. These locomotives were fitted with side window cabs and outside steam pipes. This line had a good mix of traffic with nonstop interregional trains to and from the south coast as well as local services and freight with SR, GWR and Standard locomotives all in evidence during the fifties and sixties.

SOUTH CENTRAL DIVISION • 77

Above: Excursion traffic to the south coast resorts was commonplace on summer weekends during the post-war years. This July 1960 picture, just south of East Croydon station, sees such a service from Coventry to Brighton. The motive power that day is Stanier 'Black 5' No. 45374, which was at that time allocated to Willesden shed (1A) in north London. The locomotive had been built by Armstrong Whitworth in Newcastle in June 1937 and lasted pretty much until the end of steam, being withdrawn from Carnforth shed in October 1967.

Opposite above: A basic weed killing train by 1960 now had fewer ancient tenders, these being replaced by vans and bookended by a brake van and passenger brake. This May 1960 picture at Coombe Road shows the weed killing train passing through the station behind Standard tank No. 80085 recently transferred to the Southern Region from Bletchley shed where it had been allocated from new in May 1954. There was an exchange in late 1959 that saw the SR-allocated Fairburn tanks go to the LMR, and the Standard tanks come to the SR, being allocated to Bricklayers Arms shed (73B). Derek was not a great fan of too many people in his pictures but, in this one, I am standing on the platform on the left with my 'Ilford Sporti' camera; as a mouse was to Terence Cuneo, so David Cross was to Derek Cross from time to time! Although this is no longer a Network Rail or station, some of this route is now part of the Croydon Tramlink.

Opposite below: Early June 1960 we see a brand new Brush Type 2 diesel, which had entered BR service at the end of April that same year allocated to Finsbury Park depot (34B) in north London. Looking new is No. D5604, a rare type for the Brighton line even in later years, hauling an Enfield to Brighton 'ADEX' (railway speak for a day excursion) through East Croydon, the purpose on this occasion being a day at the seaside. Such trains were commonplace at that time as very few people owned or indeed had access to cars. The rather empty street above the second carriage supports this. The train is made up of mainly maroon LNER/Gresley stock, save the penultimate coach that is in 'plum and spilt milk' livery. The loco lasted in service (as No. 31187) until 1988 and was scrapped in 1989, over thirty years ago now. A number of these Brush-built locos ran on the National Network until 2017. Many of these 1,170hp locomotives remain intact sixty years after being built in Loughborough with a number active on preserved and heritage railways.

SOUTH CENTRAL DIVISION • 79

Above: Derby Day at Epsom on 3 June 1959 sees Her Majesty the Queen travelling on board the Royal Train to Epsom race course. The train is photographed passing East Croydon. The locomotive, 'Schools' class No. 30938 *St Olave's*, has been turned out in magnificent style by the staff at its home shed of Stewarts Lane, 73A. No. 30938, designed by Maunsell, was one of twenty-one of the class fitted with the Lemaître multiple-jet blast pipe wider chimney. Forty of the class were built between 1930 and 1935 and it was frequently said that the 4-4-0 design was, by that time, obsolete. Maunsell, however, had managed to produce an outstanding and efficient design, with many people suggesting the 'Schools' class was the most powerful 4-4-0 type in Europe. I can also add – because I was curious! – that the winner of the Derby that day was a horse called *Parthia* and that the public school St Olave's was established near Tower Bridge in London and later moved to Orpington in Kent.

Opposite above: Derek did not take many pictures at the London termini. Only Waterloo and Charing Cross are featured in this book. Victoria station is so important that I had to include it and I have found a wonderful period picture from there taken in 1957. On 19 May that year an SLS special is about to set off behind a 'D1', No. 31545. On what was by all accounts a very high speed run from Victoria to East Kent, driver Sammy Gingell reportedly had the, by then, fifty-one year old 4-4-0 up to 80mph through Farningham Road en route to Shepherdswell via Margate. A pair of 'O1s' and a couple of 'R1s' toured local branches before the 'D1' hauled the 207-mile enthusiasts' special back to London's Holborn Viaduct station … full of well-dressed participants. *Transport Treasury*

Opposite below: It's been remarked on in this book before that the railways of the fifties and sixties carried a huge variety of different traffic. Pictured here at Riddlesdown in June 1960 is a troop special from Crowborough to Glasgow, a distance of just under 500 miles. The stock seems to be of mainly LMS origin and is almost certainly in maroon. The train is hauled by 'N' class No. 31412, which would have likely taken the train to Kensington Olympia before handing over to an LMR locomotive.

SOUTH CENTRAL DIVISION • 81

An evening commuter service from London to Tunbridge Wells is pictured rumbling over Riddlesdown Viaduct, three miles south of the junction at South Croydon. The train is hauled by Fairburn tank No. 42102, at that stage allocated to Tunbridge Wells West but by the end of 1959 would be based at Watford and later still sent to Springs Branch in Wigan, from where the locomotive was withdrawn in 1966.

Pictured approaching Oxted from the south we see Standard 2-6-4T and a Fairburn 2-6-4T unusually 'nose to nose' on a passenger train. Both locomotives had been built at Brighton: the Standard in 1951 and the Fairburn in 1950. This picture was taken in September 1959, just before a big swap around saw the Fairburns transferred to LMR, in this case Bletchley, being replaced by Standard tanks from the LMR to the SR. The train is a Tunbridge Wells to London service and the locomotives are No. 80014 piloting No. 42067.

SOUTH CENTRAL DIVISION • 83

The seventeen 'K' class engines, designed by Billinton and built between 1913 and 1921, were the most powerful engines on the LBSCR. Pictured here we see No. 32347 on the weed killing train near Oxted in May 1960. This locomotive remained in service until December 1962 when interestingly, and rarely, the whole class were withdrawn at the same time, reportedly for accounting reasons.

Here we see the old and the new at Oxted one summer's day in June 1959. 'E4' No. 32581, designed by Billinton and built at Brighton in 1903, sits alongside Fairburn 2-6-4T No. 42102, which had also been built at Brighton (but some forty-seven years later in 1950). The 'E4' is busy shunting the local train that went to Ashurst while the 2-6-4T is arriving at Oxted with a service from Tunbridge Wells to London. A year later both locomotives would have departed the Oxted line; the Fairburn was transferred away to Watford for use on suburban passengers in and out of London Euston and the 'E4' to Brighton shed from where it was withdrawn in early 1962.

Pictured departing from Oxted station is a service from London to Tunbridge Wells. No. 80137 had an active life of less than ten years; built in 1956, the locomotive was first allocated to Neasden shed in north London before being transferred to Tunbridge Wells West in 1959. The locomotive was withdrawn from Nine Elms shed in October 1965. After withdrawal the locomotive was scrapped at Cox & Danks at Park Royal in north London in November 1965. From build to demolition in less than ten years – such a waste!

A returning 'race special' from Lingfield Park to London is pictured approaching Oxted from the south in August 1959. Lingfield is just seven miles south of Oxted and twenty-seven miles from London Bridge. The coaching stock is a varied rake and appears to include a Pullman car as well as an interesting brake behind the locomotive. Special trains to and from race meetings were common on the British Railways of the early sixties and whether to Lingfield or Epsom tended to be made up of whatever passenger rolling stock was spare! I don't suppose the returning race goers were too fussed about the stock as long as they had a seat! The motive power that day is provided by a 'U1' class – No. 31895 of Stewarts Lane shed. Designed by Maunsell and built at Eastleigh in 1931 these three-cylinder 2-6-0s were very similar to the 'N1' class except for larger driving wheels and detail differences which allowed them to work on the Hastings line which was gauge restricted .

SOUTH CENTRAL DIVISION • 85

Still in Oxted, this time with a nice view of the signal box on the right. Behind the chimney of the locomotive Standard tank, No. 80032, we can see some of the water column and the side tanks are probably being topped up whilst the train is stationary. The train is a service from London Bridge to Brighton via Oxted and East Grinstead, a distance of little over fifty miles. In those days there were a number of routes from London to Brighton and although this was not the most direct it was perhaps the most scenic! The journey time this way between London and Brighton in July 1959 would have been just over two hours.

Pictured at Crowhurst Junction, between Godstone and Edenbridge, on the line from Redhill to Tonbridge we see a very mixed freight hauled by Maunsell 'Q' class No. 30537. The signal protecting the junction is a typical very elderly LBSCR signal. The picture was taken in March 1960. At that time No. 30537 was allocated to Norwood Junction shed, later moving to Brighton shed and ending up withdrawn from Stewarts Lane shed in December 1962.

Lots of activity in the yard at East Grinstead Low Level pictured on a fine morning in April 1960; we can see 'U1' No. 31890 and 'C2X' No. 32521. Derek records the 'U1', the first of the class rebuilt from *River Frome* in 1928, as hauling a condemned wagon special from the Bluebell Railway to Lancing wagon works whilst the 'C2X' he notes as being on yard pilot duty. The make-up of the trains seems to suggest that this is correct. No. 31890 was allocated to Brighton at this time and, after a spell at Norwood Junction, returned to Brighton in December 1962, six months before withdrawal.

Common in the fifties and sixties, but virtually unknown today, are 'Ramblers' Excursions'. Pictured at East Grinstead beside East Grinstead C signal box on 23 September 1959 is such an excursion train from London to Horsted Keynes. Horsted Keynes was the next and final stop. It is now, of course, on the heritage Bluebell Railway. The motive power that day is unrebuilt Bulleid pacific No. 34068 *Kenley*, which had been built in 1947 at Brighton and delivered new to Ramsgate shed. An early withdrawal in December 1963 from Salisbury shed, the locomotive was scrapped at Eastleigh works in March 1964, one of nine light pacifics to be disposed of there. Albeit with a different numbered Bulleid, this is one of the few scenes in the book that could be replicated sixty-three years later.

SOUTH CENTRAL DIVISION • 87

Towards the end of steam on the Southern Region it was possible to photograph former Southern Railway locomotives and BR Standard locomotives together. This picture taken in February 1960 at East Grinstead High Level sees such a combination. The train engine that day on a Groombridge to Three Bridges ballast train is BR Standard tank No. 80082, which had been built in Brighton in 1954. The pilot engine, 'E4' class No. 32581, had also been built in Brighton but some fifty-one years earlier in 1903. The fifty-year difference is nicely illustrated by the size, tractive effort and wheel arrangement that had evolved in the construction of tank engines over that exceptionally long period.

The picturesque Grange Road station in deepest West Sussex was on the branch between Three Bridges and Tunbridge Wells. Pictured we see 'M7' class No. 30055 setting off towards East Grinstead. The tail lamp on the locomotive confirms that this was a push-pull operation that ran backwards and forwards between Three Bridges and East Grinstead. The loading gauge and the coal wagons on the right indicate there was still a freight service on this cross-country Southern Railway/Region byway. This branch closed on 2 January 1967.

Pictured approaching Rowfant is a long engineers train, including a plough brake van, towards the end of March 1960. The train is double-headed by 'Q' class No. 30547 and 'C2X' No. 32544. The Maunsell 'Q' had been built just before the war at Eastleigh in 1939 and was one of class still fitted with the Lemaître large diameter chimney. Bulleid had fitted them all with these chimneys but these unfortunately corroded very easily and led to some of the locomotives being fitted with BR standard chimneys later in their lives. The train engine – 'C2X' No. 32544 – had been built nearly forty years earlier at Vulcan Foundry in December 1901. Both locomotives had been withdrawn by 1964.

A fine morning in February 1960 sees Standard tank No. 80015 pulling away from the station stop at Hartfield in East Sussex. The train is a four-coach service from London to Tunbridge Wells via East Grinstead. The lack of activity at the station seems to suggest a lack of passengers and therefore no surprise this line was closed a couple of years later. There is, however, some activity with the local coal merchant busy with some freight outside the goods shed, seen on the left.

Ashurst station in August 1959 sees a London via Oxted to Brighton train arriving at the station. Here the train would divide with the 'Schools' class and the front portion of the train continuing on to Brighton via Eridge and Uckfield. The rear portion of the train would be collected by the 'Q' class, No. 30538, waiting in the adjacent platform, before setting off to Tunbridge Wells. The main train is hauled by 'Schools' class No. 30917 *Ardingly*, which had been built in 1933 at Eastleigh. The 'Q' class was also built at Eastleigh, but five years later in 1938. Both would be withdrawn by the end of 1963.

This July 1959 picture at Ashurst Junction sees a Brighton via Oxted to London service heading towards Oxted. The southern approaches of the Brighton line to Tunbridge Wells were nothing if not complex and the key was the triangle of lines from Birchden Junction in the south to Ashurst Junction in the north-west and Groombridge to the east. Complex in those days it's not straightforward today with the heritage Spa Valley Railway and the National Network sharing Eridge station and a double single line northwards for a mile. The train is hauled by Brighton-allocated 'Schools' class No. 30901 *Winchester*.

That same January day in 1960 saw 'E4' 0-6-2T No. 32509 busy shunting the goods yard after the arrival from Eastbourne of the daily Cuckoo line pick-up goods. Adjacent to the station there was a fair size goods yard (now a fair size supermarket) with what looks like a 'C' class lurking at the other end of the yard. The Billinton-designed tank engine was already into its sixtieth year of operation and looks to be in good shape, shunting the yard on that snowy day. Some of this site (the left hand side) is now part of the preservation scene, with the Spa Valley Railway being headquartered on the site. The locomotive remained in service until March 1962.

Snow in Kent is not common and, in this view taken in January 1960, is a little half-hearted. A Brighton to Tonbridge local service is pictured approaching Tunbridge Wells West behind standard tank No. 80148. This Brighton-built loco only lasted 7½ years in service (1956-1964) and was a Southern Region 'lifer' throughout its very short working life. Only being allocated to two sheds, namely Brighton and Feltham, the locomotive was scrapped in April 1965.

Elsewhere in these pages we have seen a number of pictures of weed killing trains. It seems that in the 1959/60 period there were a number of different train sets. The more modern ones had modern four-wheel tanks of water while the older set, pictured here, had a variety of old steam locomotive six-wheeled tenders to carry the water to mix with the chemicals to be sprayed on the track. Pictured here propelling out of Eridge is 1920-built 'K' class No. 32350. The picture was taken in June 1960.

This picture at Eridge station in May 1959 sees Fairburn tank No. 42102 leaving with a local stopping service from Eastbourne to Tunbridge Wells. The locomotive at that stage was nine years old whilst the rolling stock it was pulling was probably fifty years or more older, being of LBSCR origin and in all likelihood painted bright red. Eridge today is interesting, being shared between National railway services to and from Uckfield and the heritage Spa Valley Railway to Tunbridge Wells.

Wainwright 'L' class No. 31777, one of a class of twenty-two locomotives all built in 1914, is pictured at Eridge. This example, unusually, had been built in Germany by Borsig of Berlin and assembled at Ashford. The train is a stopping service from Brighton to Tunbridge Wells and Derek has taken the picture from the signal box. In the very bottom of the right hand corner of the picture you can see a little garden that the signalman used to maintain, where some plants surround a flat brick structure spelling out Eridge. Derek often based himself in signal boxes and befriended signalmen, which allowed him to have a cup of tea, a chat and a smoke; the reward for which was often a couple of prints for the signalman at a time when very few people owned cameras.

Super power for a local train on the Cuckoo line. This May 1960 picture, taken at Hailsham station, sees a local train from Eastbourne arriving and terminating. As a result of a diagram involving an Oxted line commuter train, it was not unknown for a two-coach local to be hauled by an unrebuilt 'West Country' class pacific. This Bulleid 'West Country', No. 34019 *Bideford*, had been built at Brighton in December 1945 and for much of its working life was allocated to the former LSWR lines. However, from September 1958 until August 1963, *Bideford* was allocated to Brighton shed, hence her appearance in the Eastbourne area. Of interest, No. 34019 was one of the two 'West Country' class converted to oil firing in 1947, but then subsequently converted back to coal.

April 1960 sees a Hailsham to Eastbourne service departing from Hailsham behind unrebuilt Bulleid 'West Country' pacific No. 34098 *Templecombe*. To have pacifics on two-coach local services more than once was not uncommon in 1960 because this local train was part of a diagram using the locomotive that worked the morning and afternoon commuter train to London on the Oxted line. The trip to Hailsham was a regular filling-in turn for the pacific. Also of interest is the first coach dating back to 1900 LBSCR suburban stock and the second coach a Maunsell corridor, one in red and one in green. No. 34098 was built in December 1949 in Brighton; it was withdrawn in June 1967 from Eastleigh shed and scrapped in South Wales at Buttigiegs scrapyard in Newport in September 1968.

Passing the very impressive Polegate A signal box we see 'E4' class No. 32479 arriving at Polegate with a Cuckoo line service from Tunbridge Wells to Eastbourne. No. 32479 had been reallocated to Brighton in March 1960 and was to remain at that shed until withdrawal in June 1963. It is quite remarkable that this Billinton tank engine had been built in December 1898 and was still involved on passenger services some sixty-two years later.

Polegate was the junction for the Cuckoo line to Eridge and the main line to London and the north. Simultaneous departures are pictured on Saturday 9 July 1960, both trains being hauled by Standard tanks. On the left, behind No. 80095, is a service from Eastbourne to Tunbridge Wells and, on the right, hauled by No. 80141, a service from Hastings to Sheffield. On the latter service, the Standard tank would likely be changed at Brighton.

Polegate was quite a large station in East Sussex a few miles north of Eastbourne and on summer Saturdays in the early sixties, it was a favourite place for Derek to take pictures. Going back sixty years the resorts of the south coast, particularly east of Eastbourne, were much favoured by people in the midlands and north for their annual summer holidays. On 9 July 1960 we see one of these services departing from Polegate behind Standard tank No. 80141, at that stage only four years old. The train is an Saturdays Only service from Hastings to Sheffield.

SOUTH CENTRAL DIVISION • 95

Summer Saturday trains from Hastings and Eastbourne went to a great variety of destinations in the midlands and the north. Pictured already we have seen trains to Sheffield. There are other pictures of trains to Leicester and to Birmingham and pictured here a service from Hastings to Birkenhead. It seems that, as well as having a variety of destinations, these trains had a variety of motive power and the service to Birkenhead on 9 May 1960 was hauled by Bulleid 'West Country' pacific No. 34097 *Holsworthy*. No. 34097 had been built at Eastleigh at the end of 1949 and, when pictured, was allocated to Brighton shed. The locomotive was rebuilt in March 1961 and withdrawn from Eastleigh in April 1966.

The demise of the Bluebell line coincided with a substantial drop off in freight traffic generally. The truck had arrived! This led to the Bluebell line being used as an extremely long siding around Kingscote for the storage of condemned freight wagons. Many of these wagons were destined to be cut up at the wagon works at Lancing as well as at Newhaven. This meant that from time to time a locomotive was sent to Kingscote to fetch the next raft of wagons to go for scrap. Pictured here passing through Ardingly station in February 1960 is a condemned wagon special from Kingscote to Lancing. The motive power that day was K class, 32343 (built 1916 in Brighton) and at that time allocated to BrIghton shed, 75A.

Above: Pictured here, joining the main London to Brighton line at Copyhold Junction is another of the condemned wagon specials from Kingscote to Lancing Works. The train is hauled by Standard tank No. 80031, which is having to work hard as the branch from Horsted Keynes climbs up to the main line, seen through the bushes on the left-hand side. You can almost hear the wagons resisting the curve, the gradient and the fact they were on their final journey! No. 80031 had been built in Brighton in March 1952 and remained allocated to that shed until December 1963 before being transferred to Redhill shed for eighteen months. It was unusual for a locomotive to have only been allocated to two sheds and even more unusual that where the locomotive was built and both sheds were within thirty miles of each other.

Opposite above: Pictured on the fast lines heading south is a twelve-coach boat train from London Victoria to Newhaven Harbour. The train is hauled by one of the very early electric locomotives, No. E2001. Although fitted with a pantograph the locomotive is being powered by the third-rail supply. In the foreground is the branch to Ardingly and Horsted Keynes, which at that stage was also electrified. The line to Ardingly has subsequently been truncated to a stone terminal about a mile away from where this picture was taken. The third-rail electrification has, of course, also gone from the branch. The electric locomotive was designed by R.A. Worth and built in 1945. There were three locos in the class and they were quite successful, hence its use on a boat train, a service that was very important to the Southern Region. The type was, however, nonstandard and therefore did not survive long, although under TOPS it was allocated Class 70. The locomotive was scrapped in South Wales in August 1969.

Opposite below: Passing Christ's Hospital signal box we see an up engineers ballast train, including track panels. Probably because of the weight of the train, it is double-headed with 'C2X' No. 32534 piloting 'Q' class No. 30536. The picture was taken in April 1960. Interestingly the outline of both locomotives deserves some comment. The 'C2X', designed by Billinton and built in 1900 at Vulcan Foundry, was later then rebuilt by Marsh. Some members of the class had two domes, the second one carried the top-feed apparatus; No. 32534 during the course of its sixty-one year working life carried both variants. The 'Q' class No. 30536, photographed with a large diameter chimney, lost this in 1961 due to corrosion and gained a BR standard chimney.

SOUTH CENTRAL DIVISION • 97

No more than a month old BR Type 2 diesel, No. D5074 is pictured passing through Christ's Hospital station with an excursion from Northampton to Bognor Regis. The picture was taken in April 1960. The locomotive had been built at Derby Works in March 1960. The future Class 24s were one of the more successful 'Pilot Scheme' diesel locomotives. Built over three sites at Derby, Crewe and Darlington, only a handful of them reached twenty years in service. This example was withdrawn from Crewe in October 1975 and was scrapped by Cashmore at Great Bridge the following year.

Inter-regional services to the south coast were very common at weekends during the fifties and sixties. In the spring of 1960, we see one of these services passing Christ's Hospital; on this occasion the service is running from Bedford to Bognor Regis. The locomotive that day is Stewarts Lane-allocated unrebuilt Bulleid 'West Country' No. 34100 Appledore. This locomotive was rebuilt five months later and lasted until the end of steam on the Southern Region.

A twelve-car London to Bognor Regis electric multiple-unit heads south past Christ's Hospital in April 1960. The lead unit is '4COR' No. 3151, which had been built for the electrification of the Portsmouth main line just before the outbreak of the Second World War in 1939. The last '4COR' unit ran in September 1972.

No. 32469: the alternative *Beachy Head*. Billinton had designed his 'E4' class in the late nineteenth century and all seventy-five of these locomotives were built at Brighton between 1897 and 1903. All the 'E4's had originally been named and No. 32469 (pictured here) had been *Beachy Head*. The engines were rebuilt with Marsh boilers from 1910 onwards. This picture, taken passing Christ's Hospital B signal box, is of a service from Brighton to Horsham with a very mixed rake of rolling stock. By the time this picture was taken, in April 1960, only twenty-eight of the class remained in service and No. 32469 only lasted until October 1961 but in that time had served the LBSCR, Southern Railway and Southern Region for some sixty-three years.

Pictured near Slinfold on the railway between Horsham and Guildford we see a Horsham to Guildford service just after crossing the boundary from West Sussex into Surrey. The picture was taken in March 1960. The motive power that day was provided by an 'M7' 0-4-4T, No. 30050, which had been built at Nine Elms in June 1905, so already had fifty-five years' service with the LSWR, the Southern Railway and the Southern Region. The interesting aspect of this picture is in the coaching stock where each of the three vehicles is completely different and with very varying origins.

The first station south of Guildford on the Cranleigh branch is Bramley & Wonersh. Pictured near that station in April 1960 is an excursion from Reading to Brighton, a pretty direct route through West Sussex. The train that day is hauled by Bulleid 'Q1' No. 33022. Built during the war in 1942 the locomotive remained in service until January 1964 before being scrapped in South Wales.

The LCGB 'Wealdsman' rail tour sets off on 13 June 1965 from a photographic stop at Baynards station, the only passing place on the Cranleigh branch. The poor state of the track, the general dereliction of the goods yard and the crowd of local people on the platform all suggest this special was being run in connection with the closure of the branch that week. Motive power that day was a pair of Guildford-allocated 'Q1s', Nos. 33027 and 33006. Both of these engines had less than six months left in traffic, both being withdrawn in January 1966. These two locos and No. 33020 were the last three of the 'Q1' class in service.

That Easter holiday excursion train seen earlier at Bramley & Wonersh is pictured passing through Rudgwick station; this was a typical sixties wayside branch line station site with signal box, small goods yard and aged road lorries! Derek must have had a remarkable turn of speed from his MG Magnette to get two shots of the same train on the Cranleigh branch! The train hauled by Guildford-allocated 'Q1' No. 33022.

Above: On the Midhurst branch in West Sussex Derek has captured a 'C2X' doing some shunting in the platform at Petworth station. It would appear that the train has been split and some wagons are being detached into the station goods yard. The photograph was taken in April 1960. The 'C2X', No. 32523, had reached sixty years in operation, having been built in 1900 at Vulcan Foundry in Lancashire. Allocated, when seen here, at Three Bridges shed, the locomotive was to remain in service until February 1962.

Opposite above: The Midhurst branch again and the daily pick up goods from Midhurst to Horsham sits in the platform at Petworth station. The motive power that day in March 1960 is a Billinton 0-6-2T 'E4', No. 32469. This locomotive had been built in Brighton and put to service in June 1898; it was still looking in pretty good condition some sixty-two years later. The locomotive was withdrawn from Three Bridges shed the following year in 1961. Sister locomotive, No. 32473, now 124 years old, is the only 'E4' preserved and today operates on the Bluebell line.

Opposite below: The LCGB 'The Wealdsman Rail Tour' took place on 13 June 1965. The circular route was from Waterloo to Horsham, Three Bridges, East Grinstead, Polegate, Hastings, Eastbourne, Haywards Heath and back to London. It seems the tour was run to commemorate the closure of both the Cuckoo and Cranleigh lines, which had both closed the day before (on 12 June), as part of the Beeching axe. The motive power that day on the special around Mid-Sussex comprised two Moguls, two 'Q1s' and this rebuilt 'Battle of Britain', No. 34050 *The Royal Observer Corps*. This picture was taken near West Grinstead.

SOUTH CENTRAL DIVISION • 103

SOUTH WESTERN DIVISION

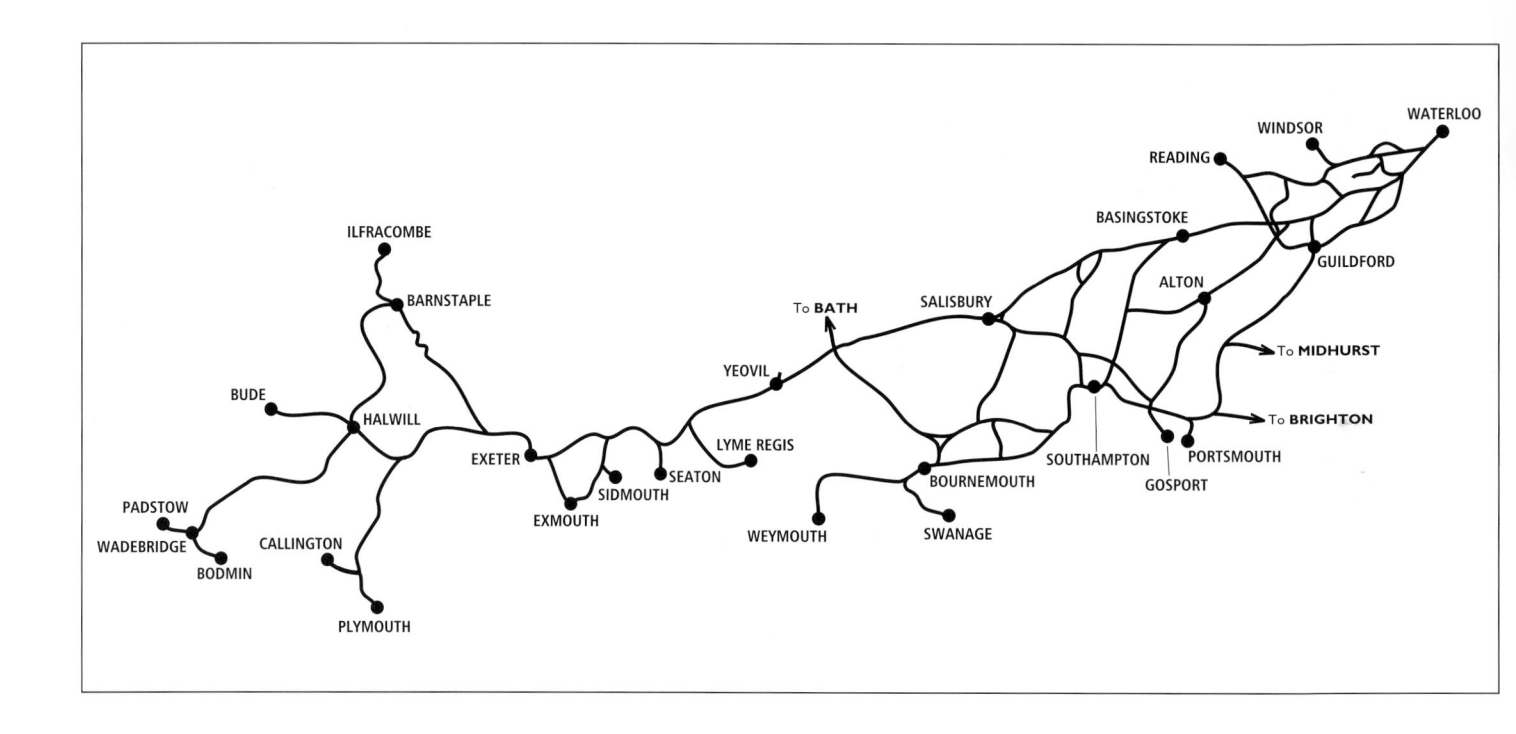

Opposite above: London Waterloo, nearly seventy-one years ago, the picture shows 'Lord Nelson' class No. 30850 *Lord Nelson* about to depart this famous LSWR terminus. Both the locomotive and the station remain with us today. The picture was taken on Derek's birthday, Friday 5 October 1951, and shows a service to Bournemouth ready to leave. The 'Lord Nelson' is flanked by a 'T9', No. 30719, on the left and a 'Remembrance' on the right. In 1951 the journey to Bournemouth would have taken about two and a quarter hours for the 108-mile journey. No. 30850 is preserved as part of the National Collection and is presently being restored at the Mid-Hants Railway at Ropley.

Opposite below: A misty foggy morning at London Waterloo on 10 February 1967. The new order is already in evidence with the end of steam on the former LSWR main line just five months away in July 1967. An inward service form Bournemouth made up of a rake of electric multiple-unit stock is pictured arriving behind BRCW Type 3 diesel No. D6554. New in May 1961 and allocated to Hither Green depot, this diesel is already six years old. The locomotive later became No. 33036 in 1974 and was withdrawn much earlier than many of the class, in July 1979, and scrapped at Slade Green later the same year. The old Art Deco signal box is prominent on the right hand side of the picture.

SOUTH WESTERN DIVISION • 105

106 • THE DEREK CROSS COLLECTION: THE SOUTHERN IN TRANSITION 1946–1966

The changeover years actually taking place! Steam traction, electric traction and diesel traction altogether at the end of the platform at Waterloo again on 10 February 1967. On the right we see rebuilt Bulleid 'Merchant Navy' class No. 35013 *Blue Funnel* (still carrying nameplates) waiting to leave with an express to Weymouth. In the distance an electric unit disappears into the winter fog on a suburban service whilst on the left 'Warship' class diesel No. D826 *Jupiter* is waiting to leave with an express to Exeter. *Jupiter* had been built at Swindon in September 1960 and was already more than half way through its life, being withdrawn in October 1971.

The cold dank February morning probably makes a, by then, not very well maintained Standard tank look in worse condition than the locomotive actually was. Engaged with an empty stock movement from the platform at London Waterloo is No. 80133 getting under way towards Clapham. No. 80133 was withdrawn just five months later in July 1967 but, in eleven short years in traffic, had worked on the LTSR serving London from another direction, as well as operating from Neath and Swansea, from Feltham and finally from Nine Elms.

An up boat train from Southampton Western Docks, confirmed by the extra luggage vans, is seen approaching Clapham Junction on a fine day in June 1960. Steam to spare and lots of coal in the tender would indicate a pretty straightforward trip on the eighty-mile journey from Southampton. 'Lord Nelson' No. 30865 *Sir John Hawkins* had been reallocated from Bournemouth shed just six months earlier to join the rest of the class at Eastleigh. No. 30865, which was slightly different mechanically to the rest of the class, was the last to be built but the first to be withdrawn in May 1961.

A couple of pictures now at Wandsworth Common, a mile or so beyond Clapham Junction on the south-western approaches to London. First we see an LMR interloper, Fowler 2-6-4T No. 42350, making its way back to the London Midland Region with a very short transfer freight from Norwood Junction to Willesden Brent. No. 42350 was one of a class of 125 locomotives and was built at Derby in 1929; it spent much of its working life in the north-west, emigrating to Willesden for four years between stints at Lostock Hall and at Birkenhead. Only fourteen members of the class made it into 1964; No. 42350 was one of them, being withdrawn from Stafford shed in June of that year.

108 • THE DEREK CROSS COLLECTION: THE SOUTHERN IN TRANSITION 1946–1966

June 1960 sees an iconic Southern express – the 'Brighton Belle' – crossing Wandsworth Common. The service is a down train from London Victoria to Brighton, a ten-car electric multiple-unit with five-car set No. 3055 leading. The 'Brighton Belle' was the only electric Pullman car train to ever run. The last titled 'Brighton Belle' ran in April 1972, well … a set is presently being restored for use on the main line at some stage in the future. We look forward to that.

The down 'Bournemouth Belle' is pictured speeding through Weybridge in June 1959, nineteen miles into the 108-mile journey to Bournemouth West. The motive power that day is rebuilt Bulleid 'Merchant Navy' class No. 35017 *Belgian Marine*. The 'Bournemouth Belle' had first run back in 1931 and continued to operate until 1967. *Belgian Marine* had been built in original form at Eastleigh in 1945; it was rebuilt in 1957 and withdrawn in 1966 from Weymouth shed.

Passing Weybridge in May 1959 we see an express from Waterloo to Weymouth. The twelve-coach rake contains both green and 'blood and custard' stock. The branch off to the left leaves the LSWR main line and heads towards Virginia Water, Ascot and Staines. The train is hauled by unrebuilt Bulleid 'Battle of Britain' class No. 34090 *Sir Eustace Missenden (Southern Railway)*. This light pacific with the unique design of nameplate had originally been a Ramsgate locomotive. Rebuilt in 1960, the locomotive remained in service until the end of steam on this line in July 1967.

'Schools' class No. 30905 *Tonbridge* is seen at Weybridge in May 1959 looking very clean. Immediately of note is the very high-sided tender to which the locomotive is attached. This tender, formerly attached to No. 30932, was self-trimming and was transferred to No. 30905 in 1958. A couple of other members of the 'Schools' class (Nos. 30912 and 30921) were attached to ex-'Lord Nelson' bogie tenders after the latter were withdrawn in 1962. The train, a Waterloo to Salisbury service, sees *Tonbridge* returning to the city where the locomotive was shedded at that time.

Setting off from Weybridge on the branch Addlestone and Chertsey is '700' class No. 30694 with the local 'pick-up goods'. The '700' class, of which there were thirty built, had been designed by Drummond in 1897 and built by Dübs & Co in Glasgow. Later rebuilt by Urie in 1928, No. 30694 was a Nine Elms engine for many years. This class had the nickname 'Black Motors'. Of note is the LSWR signal gantry in the foreground. The picture was taken in June 1959.

A very long van train from Southampton Docks to London is making good progress eastbound through Weybridge in May 1959. In Derek's notes he thinks this might have been a train of bananas but I can't confirm this. Motive power that day is Standard 5 No. 73110 a 1955 built locomotive from Derby Works. Allocated to Nine Elms, these Standard 5s were used right across the former LSWR on a variety of passenger and freight trains. Sadly this modern locomotive only had a working life of eleven years.

July 1960 at Brookwood sees a London Waterloo to Basingstoke semi-fast ambling along the fast line some twenty miles from the Hampshire town. Of interest are the third rails on both the up and down slow lines which went as far as Pirbright Junction on the route to Alton. Full electrification of the former LSWR main line did not take place until 1967, some seven years after this picture was taken. Motive power that day is 'Schools' class No. 30912 *Downside*. A long-time Ramsgate locomotive, No. 30912 was transferred to Nine Elms in May 1959 and remained there until withdrawn in December 1962. The last eighteen months in traffic saw No. 30912 running with an eight-wheeled tender from the first withdrawn 'Lord Nelson', No. 30865, in May 1961.

On 21 September 1960, west of Brookwood, we see 'T9' No. 30729, which was built by Dübs in Scotland in December 1899 and so, by this time, had been in service for sixty-one years. The train is a westbound engineers train bowling along the fast line towards Basingstoke with a wonderful equally aged train formation. The 'birdcage' brake carriage is thought to date from the 1890s, built for the LSWR. The 'T9' had a rather nomadic existence, having been allocated to six sheds since 1948 ranging from Stewarts Lane in London to Exmouth Junction where, on that day in September 1960, it was allocated. The 'T9' had worked to London with an enthusiast special the day before and was returning west to Eastleigh. Reports suggest this was the last 'T9' to work out of the London area. Six months later, in March 1961, the locomotive was withdrawn. One member of the class survives (No. 30120) from the sixty-eight that had transferred to the Southern Region in 1948. This loco has a six-wheeled tender as opposed to the eight-wheeled 'water cart' tender that a number of the class had.

Saturday 10 September 1960 sees 'Lord Nelson' class No. 30855 *Robert Blake* heading north through the cutting near Brookwood with a Salisbury to London Waterloo semi-fast; it has to be said having a rather mixed rake of passenger stock! Allocated to Eastleigh shed (71A) at the time with the rest of the class, *Robert Blake* was to remain in traffic for one more year until September 1961. The pneumatically operated signal gantry above the train, as well as being a very attractive structure, was pretty much unique. The distance from the controlling signal box was so far that normal signal wire would not work so compressed air was used instead.

A typical early sixties formation for a semi-fast from Basingstoke to London Waterloo with as many passenger vehicles as non-passenger vehicles and great variation of the latter. The first vehicle behind the tender is a 1920 built GWR Syphon van. The train is hauled by No. 30453 *King Arthur*, which carried the name after which the class was known. This February 1925 example is an 'Eastleigh' 'Arthur' as opposed to some of the class built by North British in Glasgow, known as the 'Scotch' 'Arthurs'. Seventy-four 'King Arthurs' had entered BR Southern Region stock on 1 January 1948 and, by September 1960 when this photograph was taken, east of Brookwood, there were twenty-six left in service. The story goes that this locomotive was set to be preserved as part of the National Collection but, after withdrawal in July 1961, it was scrapped rapidly just three months later. One of the class did, thankfully, survive and sister No. 30777 *Sir Lamiel* is still with us and has been an active member of the preservation scene for many years!

Summer Saturdays in the fifties and sixties often led to any locomotive that would steam being pressed into service. Lots of additional mainly Saturdays Only passenger trains were run and any locomotive available would be used. Here we see a couple of examples of this photographed at Fleet in Hampshire in July 1960. This first image sees Standard Class 4 2-6-0 No. 76026 rattling along with a Saturdays Only Lymington to London express. The Class 4 with an eight-coach load seems to be doing fine on the up fast line with thirty-six miles to go to Waterloo. The use of Standard Class 4s on this service was because the turntable at Brockenhurst could not accommodate larger locomotives. Allocated to Bournemouth shed this locomotive was to remain in service until the end of Southern Region steam in July 1967.

Unusual power again through Fleet on a summer Saturday in July 1960, this time with a down train on the slow line. A six-coach service from Waterloo to Basingstoke, twelve miles to its destination, is hauled by 'Q1' No. 33008. A long-term resident of Feltham shed, much of No. 33008's week would probably have been spent on shunting and local freight work. However, this summer Saturday in July sees the 0-6-0 pressed into passenger service. The 'Q1s' were excellent locomotives built by Bulleid during the war (1942) and would have had no problems with this outer suburban passenger train.

114 • THE DEREK CROSS COLLECTION: THE SOUTHERN IN TRANSITION 1946–1966

A lengthy goods train is seen passing through Basingstoke station after a signal check. The long mixed freight is thought to be a Feltham to Salisbury working and is hauled by 'U' class No. 31814; the locomotive was designed by Maunsell and built at Ashford in 1920. The locomotive was for a long time allocated to Salisbury (72B), making one last move to Guildford shed in August 1963 being condemned there in July 1964. The locomotive was disposed of at Cashmore's scrapyard in Newport in December 1964.

It seems that the west end of Basingstoke station has not changed too much since this picture was taken in September 1960. The LSWR signal gantry has long gone, the platform is perhaps a little longer and the lines electrified but still cross-country trains call en route to Bournemouth. This cross-country service, however, originated from a town no longer connected directly to Bournemouth, the origin of the train being Birkenhead. It was routed via Chester, Shrewsbury and Birmingham then onto the 'normal' route from the midlands. The journey time in 1960 was eight hours thirteen minutes from Birkenhead to Bournemouth West with probably three locomotive changes. The train that day is hauled by 'Lord Nelson' class No. 30858 *Lord Duncan*, which was withdrawn less than a year later in August 1961 and scrapped at Eastleigh later in the same year.

SOUTH WESTERN DIVISION • 115

Approaching Worting Junction a couple of miles west of Basingstoke we see 'King Arthur' No. 30783 *Sir Gillemere* slowing for the station stop. The train is a Bournemouth to London Waterloo service. The typical signal box, windows open on a hot summer's day in July 1960, adds to the picture with the Battledown Flyover on the left in the middle distance. Glasgow-built in 1925, this 'King Arthur' had a year left in service, being withdrawn in 1961.

Weymouth priority over Bournemouth! At Worting Junction on a summer Saturday in July 1960 we see rebuilt Bulleid 'West Country' No. 34031 *Torrington* overtaking 'Lord Nelson' No. 30861 *Lord Anson*. The Waterloo to Bournemouth train behind the 'Lord Nelson' had left Waterloo before the 'West Country' hauled Weymouth train but the Weymouth train is now given priority for the double-track section to the west towards Micheldever and Winchester. The stopping pattern of the trains probably also reflected the overtaking of the Bournemouth service.

'King Arthur' class No. 30453 *King Arthur*, built in 1925, is pictured emerging from beneath the Battledown Flyover. This long-time Salisbury-allocated locomotive is hauling a Salisbury to London Waterloo service; next stop Basingstoke. It has just passed underneath the up line from Southampton to Waterloo. The picture was taken in March 1960. Reportedly the Southern Railway was the first railway to appoint a Public Relations Officer; that appointment coincided with the delivery of this new class of passenger locomotive. The new PR man wanted names with impact and it was decided the class should be named after King Arthur and his Knights of the Round Table.

Back in June 1951 at Battledown Flyover we see 'Remembrance' No. 32333 on a service from Reading to Portsmouth. The seven locos in this class LBSCR were based at Basingstoke shed for their entire BR careers and employed on secondary services on the former LSWR, as depicted here. The background to this class, sometimes referred to as 'N15X', is an interesting one. Originally designed and built by Billinton of the LBSCR in 1914, the class began life as an 'L' class 4-6-4T, a most unusual wheel arrangement for the UK. After the Brighton line was electrified, these locos were surplus and in 1934/36 Maunsell rebuilt the class as 4-6-0 tender engines with eight-wheel tenders. Following their conversion, all were transferred to the Western Division and based at Nine Elms. All were named after locomotive engineers (Stephenson, Trevethick and Beattie, for example) whilst this loco was named *Remembrance* in memory of the men & women of the LBSCR who perished during the First World War. This black-liveried loco was withdrawn in 1956. There is a brand new replica of this locomotive currently being built at the Bluebell Railway.

June 1951 sees an inter-regional service from Bournemouth to York crossing the Battledown Flyover. The largely Eastern Region stock confirms that the destination would be in the north-east; Derek's notes say the train was going to York. The locomotive, a 'King Arthur', first of all had a wonderful name – *Joyous Gard* – as well as a double chimney, which only a handful of the class had. No. 30741 was built at Eastleigh in 1919 and allocated to Bournemouth just the year before this photograph was taken in 1950. The locomotive was withdrawn rather early in 1956. There is another north-eastern connection to this locomotive because for a year during the Second World War No. 30741 and nine sisters were transferred to Heaton shed in Newcastle to help the LNER cope with a motive power shortage and to support the war effort.

Blue Funnel in blue livery! 'Merchant Navy' class No. 35013 *Blue Funnel* is pictured passing under the Battledown Flyover in early June 1951. The locomotive, a Bulleid pacific, had been built in 1945 at Eastleigh and in 1951 was just six years old. The whole class of thirty 'Merchant Navy' pacifics were named after famous shipping lines. Some quite wonderful names from the history of British and overseas shipping lines were carried and eleven examples remain so *P & O*, *Canadian Pacific*, *Port Line*, *British India Line* and *Clan Line* have all been seen in steam in the UK since the last of the class was withdrawn by British Railways in 1967. This example is unrebuilt, the whole class having been built this way but later all were rebuilt without their streamlined casing between 1956 and 1959. *Blue Funnel* was withdrawn from Nine Elms shed at the end of Southern Region steam. Also of note is the first coach: a Maunsell open with whole windows.

A locomotive, still with us today and 100 years old, is 'S15' No. 30499, which was built at Eastleigh in 1920. No. 30499 is pictured here, seventy-one years ago in June 1951, at Battledown Flyover. Heading west on a down goods towards Salisbury, in all likelihood from west London, perhaps from Feltham yard, to the west of England, No. 30499 was, from the beginning of British Railways Southern Region, a Feltham locomotive (70B), being allocated to that shed from 1940 until withdrawal in January 1964. Now preserved at the Mid-Hants Railway it spent nineteen years at the Woodham scrapyard at Barry docks, before leaving in 1983. Estimated to have run 1.2 million miles in LSWR/SR/BR service. it is hoped it will be adding to this in Hampshire in the coming years.

Micheldever station in Hampshire, some fifty-eight miles from Waterloo, sees rebuilt Bulleid 'Merchant Navy' No. 35012 *United States Line* passing through with a Waterloo to Weymouth service in May 1960. Downhill all the way to Winchester, in fact downhill all the way to Southampton and beyond, the next gradient of any consequence is well into the New Forest between Lyndhurst Road and Beaulieu Road. Derek also photographed this locomotive on Shap, one of his other stamping grounds, on a rail tour to Carlisle.

A northbound freight is pictured on the Didcot, Newbury & Southampton line on 4 March 1960. The wartime signal box on the left tells us the location is Sutton Scotney. The train is hauled by GWR Collett goods No. 3211, which had been built at Swindon in December 1947; the locomotive had a very short life as it was withdrawn from Ebbw Junction shed in Newport during September 1962.

Although the passenger service on the DNS had ceased in March 1960 the line remained open long enough to host an LCGB excursion on 22 May 1960. This rail tour, 'The North Hampshire Downsman', complete with head board had started in London and is pictured passing through Highclere station, the nearest station to Highclere castle, now better known as Downton Abbey in the television series of the same name! The train is hauled by Wainwright-designed 'E1' No. 31067, built back in 1908 at Ashford, so with fifty-two years' service at this time. The background to the 'E1s' was very interesting as, after the First World War, the SECR had neither much motive power nor much money to provide for the fast heavy boat trains between London, Folkestone and Dover. Maunsell, by then in charge, converted ten of the class to 'E1' with super-heated boilers, new valves and new cylinders. No. 31067 was one of the ten locomotives converted by Beyer Peacock in 1921, remaining in traffic until November 1961. This locomotive accumulated the highest mileage of the 'E1s' and 'D1s' with just over two million miles run.

120 • THE DEREK CROSS COLLECTION: THE SOUTHERN IN TRANSITION 1946–1966

The last day of passenger services on the Didcot, Newbury & Southampton line was 5 March 1960. Pictured here, at Shawford Junction, where the DNS line joins the LSWR main line between Winchester and Eastleigh is, the second last train, a service from Didcot to Eastleigh. The train is hauled by Collett 0-6-0 No. 2240, built during the Second World War at Swindon and on this date allocated to Didcot shed. The viaduct on the right of the picture remains in place today with a home signal and can be seen clearly from the westbound M3 motorway as a reminder of days gone by. My business career saw me spend years in the intermodal freight and ports sector; many of us lament the closure of this line as it would have been an ideal, direct and geographically sensible way of moving containers from the Port of Southampton to the midlands and north instead of going on the circular route via Basingstoke and Reading, taking up valuable rail capacity.

That most distinctive station clock tower immediately tells us this picture is taken at Southampton Central. Departing for Waterloo on a service from Weymouth is rebuilt 'West Country' No. 34047 *Callington*. The photograph was taken on 5 October 1965 and it looks as if the first carriage might be a very early Mark 2 coach. In the background a Standard Class 4 2-6-0 is disappearing towards Southampton Western Docks.

BRITISH RAILWAYS—SOUTHERN REGION

Mail, Passenger and Cargo Services from Southampton to the Channel Islands and France—December, 1950

CHANNEL ISLANDS

OUTWARDS		INWARDS	
Mondays, Wednesdays, Fridays (Except Christmas Day)		Mondays, Wednesdays, Fridays (Except Christmas Day)	
London (Waterloo)	dep. 9.00 p.m.	Jersey	dep. 8.00 a.m.
Southampton Docks	arr. 10.51 p.m.	Guernsey	arr. 9.45 a.m.
Southampton Docks	dep. 11.45 p.m.	Guernsey	dep. 10.15 a.m.
Guernsey	arr. 6.30 a.m.	Southampton Docks	arr. 4.30 p.m.
Guernsey	dep. 7.15 a.m.	Southampton Docks	dep. 5.30 p.m.
Jersey	arr. 9.15 a.m.	London (Waterloo)	arr. 7.18 p.m.

SOUTHAMPTON - HAVRE SERVICE

OUTWARDS		INWARDS	
Mondays and Fridays (Except Christmas Day) also Tuesday, December 26th, 1950		Tuesdays and Saturdays (Except Tuesday, December 26th) also Wednesday, December 27th, 1950	
London (Waterloo)	dep. 9.00 p.m.	Havre Quay	dep. 11.00 p.m., F.T.
Southampton Docks	arr. 10.51 p.m.	Havre Quay	dep. 10.00 p.m., G.M.T.
Southampton Docks	dep. 11.15 p.m.	Southampton Docks	arr. 6.00 a.m.
Havre Quay	arr. 06.30 a.m., G.M.T.	Southampton Docks	dep. 6.48 a.m. (a)
Havre Quay	arr. 07.30 a.m., F.T.		7.03 a.m. (b)
		London (Waterloo)	arr. 8.59 a.m. (a)
			9.02 a.m. (b)

G.M.T.=Greenwich Mean Time (a) Sundays
F.T.=French Time (b) Wednesdays, except December 27th; also Thursday, December 28th.

JERSEY - ST. MALO SERVICE

Date	Jersey Dep.	St. Malo Harbour arr.	Date	St. Malo Harbour Dep.	Jersey Arr.
December	G.M.T.	F.T.	December	F.T.	G.M.T.
Thursday, 7th	10.30 a.m.	2.30 p.m. (Roadstead)	Friday, 8th	4.00 p.m.	6.30 p.m.
Thursday, 14th	06.00 a.m.	10.30 a.m.	Friday, 15th	11.00 a.m.	1.00 p.m.
Saturday, 23rd	10.30 a.m.	2.30 p.m. (Roadstead)	Saturday, 23rd	5.00 p.m. (Roadstead)	7.00 p.m.
Thursday, 28th	10.30 a.m.	2.30 p.m. ,,	Friday, 29th	09.30 a.m.	11.30 a.m.

G.M.T.=Greenwich Mean Time   F.T.=French Time

Passengers for St. Malo from the Mainland will leave Southampton by the Mail Boat on Wednesday 6th, 27th and Friday 22nd only, connecting with the departure from Jersey to St. Malo on the following day.

The extract from December 1950 shows two interesting points. Firstly, that seventy-two years ago, in a world without serious commercial aircraft, there was close co-operation between the rail companies and the shipping lines even to relatively close destinations eg St Malo and the Channel Island as this timetable shows. The second point being integrated through transport is not new! So whether the destination was 'local' or on the other side of the world, the Southern Railway/Southern Region of the fifties always provided a service.

SPECIAL BOAT TRAINS FROM WATERLOO
DECEMBER, 1950

The following are details of special boat trains arranged up to time of going to press and are liable to alteration without notice:—

Day	Date December	Vessel	Depart from Waterloo	
Thursday	7	EDINBURGH CASTLE	9.20 a.m.	10.38 a.m.
Friday	8	ORANJE	1.20 p.m.	
Friday	8	ALCANTARA	2.20 p.m.	
Friday	8	QUEEN MARY	3.24 p.m.	4.07 p.m.
			4.49 p.m.	7.00 p.m.
Friday	8	LIBERTE	1.07 p.m.	
Friday	8	ATALANTIS	8.47 a.m.	9.47 a.m.
Saturday	9	VEENDAM	4.07 p.m.	
Saturday	9	DE GRASSE	7.05 p.m.	
Tuesday	12	CARONIA	9.15 a.m.	9.47 a.m.
Tuesday	12	NIUEW AMSTERDAM	3.24 p.m.	
Thursday	14	WINCHESTER CASTLE	9.20 a.m.	10.38 a.m.
Friday	15	ARAWA	9.20 a.m.	
Friday	15	CORFU	1.07 p.m.	
Saturday	16	QUEEN ELIZABETH	11.20 a.m.	12 noon
			12.47 p.m.	
Tuesday	19	VENUS	4.00 p.m.	
Thursday	21	CAPETOWN CASTLE	9.20 a.m.	10.38 a.m.
Thursday	21	AMERICA	7.22 p.m.	
Friday	22	WASHINGTON	8.47 a.m.	
Saturday	23	ESPERANCE BAY	8.47 a.m.	
Wednesday	27	LIBERTE	1.25 p.m.	
Thursday	28	QUEEN MARY	8.20 a.m.	8.47 a.m.
			9.15 a.m.	
Thursday	28	STIRLING CASTLE	9.20 a.m.	10.38 a.m.
Saturday	30	VENUS	4.00 p.m.	

Special Train Service for Continental and Channel Islands sailings will be found on page 45

This page from the *Southampton Docks Sailing List and Shipping Guide* shows the numbers of ships using the port and the associated rail movements to and from the port. Australia, America, Southern Africa and Asian ports – eg Jakarta – were all served by rail and sea; passenger and freight all made Southampton a very important part of the 'Southern'.

A long freight from the Fawley branch – hence the oil tanks – to Eastleigh Yard is pictured ambling through Southampton Central station behind 'Q' class No. 30541. These Maunsell-designed 0-6-0s had been built with single chimneys in the late thirties and had been poor steamers. Bulleid fitted them with multiple-jet blast pipe larger chimneys, which greatly improved their performance. No. 30541 was allocated to Bournemouth shed for more than ten years; withdrawn in 1964 it was later preserved on the Bluebell Railway. Of note, on a British Railways locomotive at that time, is that there appears to be virtually no coal in the tender. I reference this as mostly empty tenders are now part of the modern heritage steam scene where budgets do not allow tenders to be full of coal, as was the case with the nationalised railway.

The afternoon of Saturday 25 June 1960 sees the Saturdays Only service from Cheltenham to Southampton Terminus leaving the penultimate stop at Southampton Central. This three-coach train would have taken just under four hours to get from Cheltenham to Southampton Terminus. The train is hauled by Churchward mogul No. 6336, which had been built in Swindon in 1921 and which at that stage was allocated to Swindon shed. This locomotive would move to Machynlleth shed in 1961 and was withdrawn in 1962.

Above: A true local service – an 'all stations' from Eastleigh to Bournemouth – emerges from the darkness of the tunnel just to the east of Southampton Central station. Motive power that day in June 1960 was 'T9' class No. 30117. This locomotive was built at Nine Elms in July 1899. Designed by Drummond, the 'T9s' were nicknamed 'Greyhounds'. When built they were involved in some of the fast express workings between London and the west of England. No. 30117, after sixty-one years of active service, is now engaged in more mundane work, a sixteen-stop local service through the New Forest to Bournemouth. What better way to spend a June afternoon!

Opposite above: June 1960 sees a Portsmouth to Bristol service leaving Southampton Central station. Passing under that wonderful signal gantry and in front of the Art Deco signal box on the left, the train is hauled by Standard Class 5 No. 73087. This BR Standard had been built at Derby in 1955 and spent its entire short working life of just eleven years – it was withdrawn in 1966 – based on the Southern Region and at Bath (Green Park) on the Somerset & Dorset. During that short time the locomotive was allocated to seven sheds and also acquired the name *Linette*. A number of these reliable and popular 4-6-0s were given ex-'King Arthur' names (on the latter's withdrawal) for a number of years in the early sixties.

Opposite below: Accelerating away from Southampton Central station in the spring of 1959 we see rebuilt Bulleid 'Merchant Navy' No. 35010 *Blue Star*. The train is a Weymouth to Waterloo service; next stop Winchester. *Blue Star* had been built in 1942 and was rebuilt in early 1957. Under two years later the ex-works livery has well and truly gone and the locomotive looks rather scruffy! The 'Merchant Navy' was allocated to Bournemouth shed (71B) at that time. Withdrawn from Bournemouth shed in late 1966, *Blue Star* survives into preservation. The locomotive is now located at the Colne Valley Railway in Essex and is a long-term restoration project. *Blue Star* is one of eleven members of the class to survive.

SOUTH WESTERN DIVISION • 125

Above: By 1966 the transition of Britain's railways from steam to diesel was well underway. Here at Southampton Central station on 3 January 1966 we see a modern diesel locomotive standing beside a steam age water column. The train is a Bournemouth to Manchester service hauled by a then two-year old Brush Type 4 diesel No. D1683, built at Loughborough in October 1963. Later Class 47 No. 47485, this locomotive had a thirty-year life, being condemned and scrapped in the 1990s over twenty-five years ago now. Again several members and variants of a class that numbered 512 locomotives remain in frontline service today, approaching their sixtieth year.

Opposite above: The Maunsell 'U' class 2-6-0s were born out of an earlier 2-6-4T design known as the 'K' class of 1917. All named after Rivers, they worked on suburban services around the capital's SECR network. In 1927 one of the class was involved in a bad accident at St Mary Cray. This resulted in the whole class being withdrawn and, as a consequence of this, the decision was taken to convert the class to 2-6-0 tender engines. This locomotive, No. 31809, the last of the class and formerly *River Dart* was rebuilt in 1928 and employed on Southern Railway semi-fast and cross-country workings thereafter. On one such working at Southampton Central in June 1959, No. 31809 is pictured departing on a service from Portsmouth to Cardiff, probably hauling the train as far as Salisbury.

Opposite below: A summer's day in June 1959 sees a Waterloo to Bournemouth express departing from Southampton Central station on the last leg of the 108-mile journey from London to the Dorset resort. Common on these services at that time were the 'Lord Nelson' class and No. 30852 *Sir Walter Raleigh* heads the train passing the Art Deco Southampton Central signal box. This class, which numbered sixteen 4-6-0s built between 1926 and 1928, were all named after famous naval commanders. Rebuilt by Bulleid in 1938 they remained popular and efficient locomotives and from late 1958 until withdrawal in 1961/62. The whole class was based at Eastleigh, regularly working these services. No. 30852 was withdrawn in February 1962 and, unusually, was scrapped at Ashford Works in the spring of 1962.

SOUTH WESTERN DIVISION • 127

Above: Upwey & Broadway station (renamed from Upwey Junction in January 1952) is about two miles from the terminus at Weymouth and more or less in the middle of the steep climb from the Dorset resort to the summit at Bincombe Tunnel. The gradient should not present much of a problem for 'King Arthur' class No. 30782 *Sir Brian*. The train is a Weymouth to Bournemouth stopping service and was recorded on a dull day in August 1961. The thirty-four-mile journey to Bournemouth would probably call at fourteen stations and the three-coach set, standard for such a service, would have carried passengers, parcels, mail and milk as the milk churn on the opposite platform confirms. *Sir Brian*, one of the Scotch 'Arthurs', was built in Glasgow in 1925, so already had thirty-six years of Southern Railway and Southern Region service. Allocated to Bournemouth shed in 1951, withdrawal came in September 1962.

Opposite above: 'King Arthur' class No. 30805 *Sir Constantine*, of 1927 vintage, is pictured at Upwey Wishing Well Halt, about to stop with a two-coach local from Weymouth to Dorchester West – super power indeed for a seven-mile journey! The picture was taken in September 1959; No. 30805 was, at that time, allocated to Eastleigh, from where the locomotive was withdrawn and scrapped before the end of the same year. In the introduction I mentioned Derek's photographic trips were well-planned affairs and here above the first coach on the other side of the railway my brother and I sit dutifully watching the trains go by.

Opposite below: The ten-coach express for London Waterloo has set off from Weymouth and is pictured approaching Upwey Wishing Well Halt, a couple of miles into the 147-mile journey to the capital. That day in July 1960 the power is provided by a pair of Standard Class 5s, No. 73031 piloting No. 73085. These were both Derby-built examples of the successful Riddles designed class. The Standard Class 5s reached all over the BR network and this pair rather proves the point, with No. 73031 being allocated to Bristol Barrow Road and No. 73085 to Nine Elms shed in London. Of interest, the former had been allocated to the Rugby testing plant for almost a year in 1958 and the latter was later named *Melisande*.

SOUTH WESTERN DIVISION • 129

Above: A southbound parcels train is pictured passing through Upwey Wishing Well Halt very close to the end of its journey into Weymouth. Taken on 23 July 1960, the parcels service is rather unusually hauled by GWR 2-8-0 No. 3865, which was at that time allocated to Oxley shed in Wolverhampton. Surprisingly for Derek, who was normally meticulous, he does not state the origin of this service. The first vehicle looks like a 'blue spot' fish van, perhaps not surprising on a service destined for Weymouth. The locomotive, a Churchward designed freight engine, had been built during the war at Swindon and put into service at Swindon in November 1942. No. 3865 was the penultimate member of the class and, also of interest, was one of nineteen locomotives converted to oil firing in 1947 after a protracted strike in the coalmines. By 1950 this locomotive and the others had been returned to coal burning; when reconverted, the locomotive was also returned to No. 3865 from her oil burning identity as No. 4851.

Opposite above: The first 4½ miles away from the sea at Weymouth was a ferocious climb, especially from a standing start. Pictured here passing through Upwey Wishing Well Halt (a wonderful name for a station) into the last stage of the climb, at this stage 1 in 50, easing through the station, before reaching the summit at Bincombe Tunnel signal box, about a mile away is a Weymouth to Wolverhampton returning holiday train, and how do we know this? Three of the first four coaches are BSKs, suggesting an excursion set and 20 July 1963 was a summer Saturday, even though that part of Dorset that day appears rather grey. The 'Grange' class No. 6825 *Llanvair Grange* had spent most of its life in Cornwall but transferred to Reading in September 1962, so no surprise to find it employed on such a service a year later. The banking engine is Standard Class 5 No. 73021, a Gloucester locomotive at the time, which would probably, after banking this train, run back to Weymouth to work a later service back to the midlands.

Opposite below: By the summer of 1964 the Bulleid pacifics that had held sway on the former LSWR lines for some years were being usurped by modern traction and locomotives cascaded from other areas. This led to pacifics undertaking more menial tasks and this photograph taken on 8 June that year proves the point. Here rebuilt 'West Country' No. 34012 *Launceston* is pictured setting off from the Semley stop on a Salisbury to Exeter local service. It is eighty-eight miles from Salisbury to Exeter so a very lengthy local service with close on twenty station stops in those days over fifty-five years ago now. *Launceston* had been Brighton-built in 1945 and was withdrawn from Bournemouth in 1965 – an active life of just twenty years.

SOUTH WESTERN DIVISION • 131

Above: On Monday 8 June 1964 at Semley in Wiltshire we see Standard Class 4, 2-6-0 No. 76008 departing the station with a Gillingham to Salisbury school special. You might ask why arrange a special train for a journey of twenty-one miles each way? In those days there was much less reliance on road transport and both school specials and short rail journeys were commonplace. There is a fair assumption that, once the children had visited Salisbury Cathedral and other attractions, they would return back to Dorset the same way. No. 76008, a Riddles design, was built at Horwich in 1953. It was initially allocated to Eastleigh; however, much of its short fourteen-year existence was spent allocated to Salisbury shed (first 72B and later 70E).

Opposite above: Timeless 1950s Britain! Pictured in the terminus at Lyme Regis on a hot August afternoon in 1957 we see Adams radial tank, No. 30583. This locomotive, preserved at the Bluebell Railway today, has a fascinating history. Built as one of a class of seventy-one locomotives, this example was built by Neilson in Glasgow in March 1885. Many of her sister locos were withdrawn as long ago as 1916. By 1928 only two examples remained and a long way from their initial work on suburban passenger lines around south London. No. 30583's two sisters were based at Exmouth Junction shed to work the Lyme Regis branch. This branch line was steep and curved and these Adams locomotives were very suited to the line. The future No. 30583 had been sold to the Ministry of Munitions in 1917 and later to the East Kent Railway in 1919. The Southern Railway found the other two Adams tanks were too few to operate the line to Lyme Regis and so bought the locomotive back from the EKR and despatched it to Exmouth Junction. Here in 1957 the locomotive, already seventy-two years old and on a scheduled passenger service, waits at Lyme Regis before setting off back up the branch to Axminster just over six miles away. These three ancient Adams radial tanks were replaced by Ivatt tanks in 1961, but only because the Western Region had taken over that part of the West Country and wished to stamp their authority on this branch and a number of others in Dorset … and in Somerset!

Opposite below: The first Class M7, No. 30021, built at Nine Elms in January 1904, is pictured fifty-five years later in the station at Seaton Junction in Devon in September 1959. No. 30021 was a bit of a nomad and since January 1948 had been allocated to Bournemouth, Horsham and Guildford before fetching up at Exmouth Junction in March 1951 and eight years later was still pottering up and down the track from Seaton Junction to Seaton. As pictured, the branch line train is just arriving from Seaton some 4¼ miles distant. The ancient rolling stock both on the train and in the siding, as well as the station furniture and period clothes, all add to the rather typical picture of a British Railways Junction station in the late fifties. Both Seaton and Seaton Junction stations are closed now – the branch closed on 7 March 1966 – and the now single-track main line is all that remains.

SOUTH WESTERN DIVISION • 133

Above: Seaton Junction again and here the down 'Atlantic Coast Express' is pictured passing through the station with the locomotive change and train split in Exeter just twenty-four miles distant. At this stage, through Seaton Junction station, the gradient stiffens from 1 in 100 to 1 in 80 on the way to the summit at Honiton. Passing the very distinctive and unusual LSWR signal is rebuilt 'Merchant Navy' pacific No. 35016 *Elders Fyffes*, then allocated to Nine Elms shed. Perhaps the most unusual name amongst a class of shipping companies, Elders Fyffes was a shipping company formed in 1901, concerned principally with moving bananas from the Caribbean. Elders Fyffes Ltd was a subsidiary of Elder Dempster Line (after which company No. 35030 was named), so two of the class were named after related shipping lines.

Opposite above: The premier daily service on the Southern Region main line to the West Country was the 'Atlantic Coast Express', which ran between Waterloo and Plymouth. Pictured here is the up service from Plymouth to Waterloo passing on the through lines at Seaton Junction in September 1959, behind 'Merchant Navy' pacific No. 35026 *Lamport & Holt Line*. The locomotive, locally-allocated at Exmouth Junction shed, would have come onto the train at Exeter Central for the 172-mile journey to London Waterloo. From Exeter the former LSWR route is steeply graded initially, culminating after eighteen miles or so at Honiton Tunnel. After that the six miles to Seaton Junction is steeply downhill so the up 'ACE' is probably travelling fast, the locomotive blowing off clearly has steam to spare. No. 35026 remained in service until March 1967 when withdrawn from Weymouth shed and scrapped later that year in South Wales, where fifteen of the 'Merchant Navy' class met their end.

Opposite below: A Yeovil to Exeter semi-fast is pictured ambling through the beautiful Devon countryside near Honiton on a late summer afternoon in September 1959. The train is hauled by 'S15' No. 30824. The locomotive was built in 1927 at Eastleigh and was one of the class fitted with an eight-wheel tender from new. No. 30824 was allocated to Salisbury shed at this time and had been since 1951. Withdrawn in 1965, by which date the locomotive was allocated to Eastleigh shed.

SOUTH WESTERN DIVISION • 135

In July 1958 we see an Exmouth to Exeter local train approaching Exeter Central station from the east. The Standard classes, the majority of which were built in the early fifties, increasingly took over from pre-grouping locomotives as the decade progressed. New to Exmouth Junction shed from building at Swindon in August 1952, 2-6-2T No. 82017 remained in the Exeter area until September 1962 before moving on to Eastleigh.

This photograph shows the approach to Exeter Central station on 7 September 1954. The extensive yards are almost as interesting as the train as the latter struggles up the 1 in 37 from Exeter St David's station. In the yard is a great variety of stock, the Pullman cars on the left probably the most interesting and I believe to be from the recently withdrawn 'Devon Belle' services. The aged parcels van on the right is also of note with its Eastern Region origins. The train is a service from Okehampton to Waterloo hauled by unrebuilt 'Battle of Britain' class No. 34053 *Sir Keith Park*. Rebuilt in 1958, No. 34053 remained in service until October 1965 when withdrawn from Bournemouth shed. In the fifty-six years since withdrawal this locomotive, in rebuilt form, has had a second life in preservation. In 2020 No. 34053 moved to be based at the Spa Valley Railway at Tunbridge Wells, just thirty-three miles from where the locomotive had been built at Brighton in 1947.

A wonderful scene at Exeter Central A signal box in July 1958. A passenger pacific stands in the platform, whilst a tank engine – we think 'E1R' No. 32124 of 1878 vintage – is busy in the yard on the right and 'S15' No. 30827 passes through with a loaded ballast train from Meldon Quarry to Exmouth Junction. Even the signalman has come to the window of the box to admire this typical fifties scene. No. 30827, one of the class upgraded by Maunsell from the original Urie design, was built in 1927 and remained in traffic until being withdrawn from Salisbury shed in 1964.

Above: Derek was a great exponent of the train in the landscape form of photography. He thought that his geological training had influenced this. In this picture it's not the geology but the man-made viaduct that dominates. Just coming off the viaduct at Calstock is an Ivatt 2-6-2T, No. 41302, hauling the Bere Alston local. The Callington branch was truncated to Gunnislake in November 1966. Since then the remaining railways have been known as the Tamar Valley line. Allocated to Plymouth Friary shed, the then seven-year-old loco (built at Crewe in 1952) remained in Devon, being later allocated to Laira and then Exmouth Junction until withdrawal in November 1963.

Opposite above: The Southern Region disc head code suggests a London to Plymouth service. Three coaches seems a light loading for such a service; however, a characteristic of Southern Region trains to the west was that often a train setting off from Waterloo might have several destinations (or portions as they were called in railway language). Yeoford is 184 miles from Waterloo and, in this case, Exeter, Ilfracombe and Plymouth may all have had a portion of the main train, hence this apparently light load. The motive power that day was 'T9' No. 30711, built in faraway Glasgow by Dübs & Co in June 1899. It rather looks like the locomotive might be running with a bigger tender, perhaps acquired from an earlier Drummond class, since withdrawn. Yeoford, on the steeply graded route, was the junction for the line to Barnstaple and Ilfracombe, which diverged there from the LSWR line to Plymouth Friary some forty-eight miles away. The principal stations on the remainder of the journey would be Okehampton and Tavistock before reaching its destination.

Opposite below: For generations the rail routes west from London towards Plymouth were much fought over by the Great Western Railway and by the London & South Western Railway and their successors. Pictured we see a Southern Region service from Waterloo to Plymouth passing Yeoford station in July 1951. Some eleven miles north-west of Exeter, Yeoford is the start of twenty miles of climbing, culminating in the four miles from Okehampton to Meldon at 1 in 77. The LSWR signal box on the right watches over the goods yard and main line as 'West Country' class No. 34030 *Watersmeet* passes with the Plymouth-bound express. Built at Brighton in 1946, this Bulleid light pacific was only five years old when the picture was taken. The locomotive remained in service until 1964, was never rebuilt and was withdrawn from Exmouth Junction shed after just eighteen years of service.

SOUTH WESTERN DIVISION • 139

Above: Deep in north Cornwall, now on the so called 'withered arm' lines, we are at Otterham station in September 1959. Standing in the platform we see 'T9' No. 30715 on the stopping service between Padstow and Exeter. This two-coach local service, plus inevitable parcels vans, is about to set off towards Tresmeer, Egloskerry and then Launceston. The branch, which never achieved the importance the LSWR had hoped for, ran for forty-seven miles between Padstow and Halwill Junction. The line was closed by the Western Region in two parts: on 3 October 1966 from Otterham and finally the whole line on 30 January 1967. Much of the line now forms part of the Camel Cycle Trail.

Opposite above: Pictured leaving Padstow station, passing the turntable and water tower and adjacent to the beach, 'T9' No. 30715 sets off for Exeter, with one of the four daily trains over the North Cornwall line that meandered for close on fifty miles across north Cornwall to Halwill Junction. The picture was taken in the late summer of September 1959. Fish had once formed regular traffic from Padstow but, by the late fifties, this had been lost to road transport and the passenger service itself was closed in 1967. The site of the station is now mostly a car park for the town, which has become a bit of a 'foody' destination in recent times with restaurants owned by Rick Stein and Paul Ainsworth to name just a few. We also understand there is a plan to have a little railway museum on part of the former railway station site … and I've got some pictures to start them off!

Opposite below: The most famous structure on the North Cornwall line is probably the bridge over Little Petherick Creek, just a couple of miles short of the branch terminus at Padstow. It is a beautiful setting, captured here by Derek one fine late summer afternoon in September 1959. The creek being crossed is itself an inlet from the nearby Bristol Channel. 'T9' No. 30715, designed by Drummond, was built in Scotland by Dübs in June 1899. Just under two years after the date of this photograph, in June 1961, the locomotive was withdrawn from Exmouth Junction shed and scrapped almost at once the following month at Eastleigh works. No. 30715 had been in service for sixty-two years.

SOUTH WESTERN DIVISION • 141

It's Cornwall in September 1959 and deep in china clay territory, we see a mixed freight arriving from Boscarne Junction at Wenford Bridge. The freight appears to be a mixture of general merchandise and china clay wagons, and even a 'modern' container is part of this lengthy train pulled by a very small locomotive built in May 1874. The Beattie Well tank was one of three members of the '0298' class (of the twelve built) that survived sixty-five years after the rest of the class had been withdrawn from London suburban duties. Nos. 30585-87 were kept for years to work the Wadebridge to Wenford Bridge mineral railway that had restricted gauge and height restrictions. No. 30585, now in 2022 some 148 years old, is preserved at Quainton Road in Buckinghamshire.

A long eastbound freight from Barnstaple to Exeter arrives into Copplestone during the summer of 1959. The locomotive that day, now some sixty-three years ago, was '700' class No. 30691, which had been built by Dübs in Glasgow in March 1897. The locomotive was withdrawn from Exmouth Junction shed in July 1961.

SOUTH WESTERN DIVISION • 143

Pictured ambling through the North Devon countryside just outside of Mortehoe we see 'N' class No. 31838 (built at Ashford in July 1924) with an Exeter to Ilfracombe freight. The picture was taken in September 1959 and illustrates nicely the fifties' railway on the Southern Region ... pristine permanent way, the period telegraph poles and a thirty-five year old locomotive on a train that will get to Ilfracombe eventually!

Unrebuilt Bulleid light pacific No. 34060 *25 Squadron* is pictured setting off from Ilfracombe in early September 1959. The train is a service from Ilfracombe to Exeter Central, a distance of around fifty-five miles and characterised by the start from the end of the platform at Ifracombe, three miles at 1 in 36! A long-time resident of Exmouth Junction, No. 34060 was rebuilt in November 1960 and remained in service until the end of Southern Region steam in 1967.

A Padstow to Bodmin service is pictured at Wadebridge service in September 1959. The motive power that day is an Adams 'O2' class, No. 30199. A veteran loco by then having been built at Nine Elms back in June 1891, it looks fine and comfortably in charge of the local passenger service. In the background that day the station pilot is Beattie Well Tank No. 30586 resting in the goods yard.

July 1958 sees a Brighton to Plymouth service a few yards from destination on the approach to Plymouth. The train had taken 6½ hours from Brighton and that day hauled by unrebuilt Bulleid 'West Country' No. 34035 *Shaftesbury*. A post-war product of Brighton Works in July 1946, No. 34035 was one of the first Bulleids to be withdrawn, in June 1963 from Exmouth Junction shed. The 'West Country' had worked in the west of England since 1950 and as compared to other Bulleids in Derek's collection was very 'camera shy'!